SHOULD A CHRISTIAN BE A MASON?

E. M. Storms

Impact Christian Books

Should A Christian Be A Mason? By E. M. Storms
ISBN # 0-89228-141-3

15th Printing: 1999

Copyright © 1980, by E. M. Storms
Published by :
Impact Christian Books, Inc.,
332 Leffingwell Ave.,
Kirkwood, MO 53122

Footnoted material in this book is reprinted by permission of several publishers which have requested acknowledgment here:

1964 American Heritage Publishing Company, Inc. Reprinted by permission from *the Horizon History of Christianity*.

Excerpts from *Two Be One*, Ernest H. J. Steed, Copyright 1978 by Logos International. Reprinted by permission of Logos International Fellowship, Inc., Plainfield, New Jersey.

Excerpts from *the Way of Witches* by Perle Epstein, Copyright 1972 reprinted by permission of Doubleday and Co., Inc.

Library of Congress Card Number 80-83598

Printed in the United States of America

This volume is dedicated to
Jesus Christ,
who alone is Truth.
Everything that contradicts His Word is error.
It is written for those who are lovers of Truth.
It is a part of a small effort
to reveal the systems
and philosophies that displace
Christianity and are destructive
to the Gospel of Grace.

E.M.S.

Foreword

I have read this work with great interest, and I am sure many others also will be edified by its content. Having left Freemasonry after 19 years and attaining the 33rd degree, I feel that a Blood-washed Christian has a duty to warn others to avoid the satanic trap of Freemasonry. Also the Mason who professes to be a Christian should leave this heresy. Mrs. Storms has researched long hours on this material; her reward will be great when she hears that, through her efforts, many are coming out of Masonry.

I believe she sets forth clearly and distinctly the thought-provoking material she has gathered. I believe the right understanding of this subject will be a blessing to many.

May it be a means of glorifying our Lord Jesus Christ.

Rev. Jim Shaw

Rev. Jim Shaw
Silver Springs, Florida

Acknowledgements

Many thanks to those who were aware of this endeavor and prayed for me during the long hours of writing and typing of this manuscript. Special thanks to my husband, Gene Kline, Ralph and Ethel Stevanus for their encouragement. Thanks to my mother, father, brothers and sisters for praying for God's guidance in my life. Heart-felt gratitude is extended to Peter Marshall who made me aware of my own idolatry while I was preparing this manuscript.

In nearly all cases, *italics found in the footnoted quotations have been added by the author or editor.* Rather than interrupt the reader in the context, we are noting that here. Parentheses added by the author are noted by brackets, not parentheses, in the footnoted material.

Table of Contents

*(Placed just before the back cover, it is suitable
for removal, photocopying, and wide distribution!)*

"Organized secrecy invites suspicion."[1]

CHAPTER 1

Compromise for the Christian

Secret societies, in former years, have been considered by the Christian to be contrary to the teaching of Christ. Jesus Christ himself said, "I spoke openly to the world . . . in secret have I said nothing" (John 18:20). However, many Christians, even clergy, belong to an organization of secrecy. Freemasonry, as it is called, is a subversive, anti-Christian movement with its roots deeply buried in occult teachings. While professing respect for Christianity, it secretly seeks to destroy it. If this position is startling, prayerfully study the following pages. Here light is rendered upon the spots and blemishes of this organization.

My resources? Numerous Masonic books, including Albert Pike's *Morals and Dogma,* found in the attic of the home of my husband's deceased grandfather who was not a Mason and had refused to join. This book apparently belonged to the former owner of the house.

Any "brother" desiring to become a member of a Lodge must apply by petition, either in writing or using the standard form of petition supplied by the Lodge. The petitioner respectfully prays ". . . that I may be initiated into the mysteries of Freemasonry . . ."[2] What are the mysteries of Freemasonry? What is it into which the unsuspecting Christian is desiring to be initiated?

According to the *Morals and Dogma of Freemasonry*, Masonry is ". . . a successor of the Mysteries . . ."[3] and "is identical with the ancient Mysteries."[4] As revealed in *An Encyclopedia of Freemasonry* written by thirty-third degree Albert Mackey, the Ancient Mysteries were:

> . . . the secret worship rites of the Pagan gods. Each of the pagan gods had, besides the public and open, a secret worship paid to him, to which none were admitted but those who had been selected by preparatory ceremonies called Initiation.[5]

This fact, that the mysteries were secret worship rites, is supported by the Masonic degree, "Chief of the Tabernacle."

> Among the ancient Nations there was, in addition to the public worship, a private one styled the Mysteries; to which those only were admitted who had been prepared by certain ceremonies called initiations. The most widely disseminated of the ancient worships were those of Isis, Orpheus, Dionusos, Ceres and Mithras.[6]

Isis was the pagan god of Egypt. In Persia there was the worship of Mithras. In Thrace they celebrated the Cabiric Mysteries. Syrians worshiped the god Adoni in the Adonisian Mysteries and the god Dionysos was celebrated in Greece.

> The mystery religions were so called because their rites were not disclosed to the uninitiated. Most of them had in common the dying and rising of a god. The dying and rising of the god usually coincided with the fall and spring equinoxes. All the cults had fertility elements . . . In the performance of their rites men were assured that like nature, they too would be reborn after death, and that through union with the risen god they would themselves be made divine and thereby immortal.[7]

Alexander Hislop states in his work *The Two Babylons* that:

> . . . in all essential respects, these "Mysteries" in the different countries were all the same. . . . Babylon was the primal source from which all these systems of idolatry flowed . . . . [8]

If Freemasonry is a *successor of,* and is *identical to* the Ancient Mysteries, as claimed, we can only conclude that the candidate for initiation into the mysteries of Freemasonry is also a candidate for initiation into the Ancient Mysteries which were *the secret worship rites to pagan gods:*

> . . . practiced in the darkness of night and often amid the gloom of impenetrable forests and subterranian caverns . . . . [9]

If this theory is true, why then does the Christian forcefully uphold Freemasonry and its teachings as Christian? *Deception is the ruling principle of Masonry.* Granted, Masonry talks much of moral excellency.

3

However, moral excellency does not necessarily identify an organization as Christian. Practically every pagan religion and cult has its own moral code and ethical standards which stress right conduct — unselfishness, tolerance, brotherly love and kindness — all the cardinal virtues.

But, under this *pretense* of moral excellency, Masonic teachings are diametrically opposed to Christianity. Satan never appears in all his grossness all at once. Instead, he inches in secretly, under false pretenses. Then the Church, in a hypnotized, back-slidden state, fails to recognize his cunning and tolerates his corruption. To do this, Satan skillfully unites idolatry and paganism with Christianity while nominally admitting Christian terms and Christian names. This is precisely what has been done through Freemasonry.

At this point enthusiastic Masons will be objecting strenuously, stating that the Masons believe in God and the Bible. And it is just this bait that attracts the Christian and ensnares him.

It is requested of the candidate into Masonry that he declare his belief in *a* Supreme Being. The Christian, of course, believes that it is his Triune God, through Jesus Christ, that all Masons believe in and worship. However, to declare one's belief in a Supreme Being is *not* unique to Christianity. It is merely what is termed "theism." Even polytheism asserts that there is one Supreme Being over all the other gods. And the initiate in the Ancient Mysteries (that corrupt pagan worship) was taught the existence of a Supreme Being.

The ancient Babylonians, just as the modern Romans, recognized in *words* the unity of the Godhead; and while worshiping innumerable deities, they distinctly acknowledged that there was ONE infinite and Almighty Creator, supreme over all.[10]

In the early ages of mankind the existence of a sole and omnipotent Diety, who created all things, seems to have been the *universal belief;* and tradition taught men the same notions on this subject, which, in later times, have been adopted by all civilizations.[11]

It is apparent in Masonry that it does not matter what ideas or images you conjure up of God, just so you believe in *a* God. This is definitely contrary to Christian thinking because *our personal concept of God is worthless unless it coincides with His revelation of Himself through Jesus Christ.*

That Masonry is not concerned with one's own concept of God is indicated by the teachings of the degree of "Elu of Fifteen."

. . . opening wide its portals, it invites to enter there and live in peace and harmony, the Protestant, the Catholic, the Jew, the Moslem; every man who will lead a truly virtuous and moral life, love his brethren, minister to the sick and distressed and believe in the ONE, All-Powerful, All-Wise, everywhere Present God, Architect, Creator and Preserver of all things . . .[12]

From the degree of "Royal Arch of Solomon" there comes this teaching:

The supreme, Self-existent, Eternal, All-wise, Allpowerful, Infinitely Good, Pitying Beneficient and

Merciful Creator and Preserver of the Universe was the same by whatever name he was called . . . [13]

Among *all* the ancient nations there was one faith and one idea of Deity for the enlightened, intelligent, and educated and another for the common people. To this rule the Hebrews were no exception. Yehovah, to the mass of the people, was like the gods of the nations aound them, except that he was the *peculiar* God, first of the family of Abraham, of that of Isaac, and of that of Jacob, and afterward the National God; and, as they believed, *more powerful* than the other gods of the same nature worshiped by their neighbors . . . [14]

This degree goes on to explain how distorted the Hebrew's notion of God was because they believed He required and insisted on sacrifice and burnt offerings; He was angry and jealous and revengeful; He commanded Moses and did shocking and hideous acts of cruelty and barbarity; He hardened Pharaoh's heart, etc. It states that this was not the idea of God to the intellectual and enlightened among the Hebrews. Men like Zoroaster, Menu, Confucius, Socrates and Plato possessed a knowledge of the true nature and attributes of God, but did not make it known to the masses because of their feeble intellects. But this true knowledge of God, and other secrets, are supposedly now being passed down in Masonry and are being made known to the Grand Elect, Perfect and Sublime Masons. This degree also teaches the different names for God, including the names Bal, Bala, Molech and Malek. Thus it equates the God of the Hebrews with these heathen deities!

Lest the reader be still unconvinced that Masonry equates the Christian God with the heathen abominations, let us listen to the instruction given in the degree of "Knight Rose Croix."

> The God of nineteen-twentieths of the Christian world is only Bel, Moloch, Zeus, or at best Osiris, Mithras, or Adonai, under another name, worshiped with the old Pagan ceremonies and ritualistic formulas. It is the Statue of Olympian Jove, worshiped as the Father, in the Christian Church that was a Pagan Temple; it is the Statue of Venus, become the Virgin Mary.[15]

What an affront to Christianity! We simply cannot lay our Christian faith along side the others and consider it equal with them, nor can we believe that our God and Saviour, Jesus Christ, is represented by any name given him in the pagan faiths.

> Jesus Christ is either the only Saviour of the world, or He is not a Saviour at all, but only a religious genius. The essence of Christianity, according to the Bible, consists not in its incidental affinities with other religions, but in its distinctive elements. The Gospel is related to other faiths as either-or. We cannot simultaneously affirm: there is salvation in none other; and the others, Buddha, et al., represent the same thing as Jesus, only perhaps a bit less perfectly.[16]

The "Royal Arch" degree describes the "lost" name of God as JAH-BUL-ON, or J.B.O., and Masons of this degree have sworn never to reveal it. It simply means thus:

J — (Jehovah) Hebrew
B — (Baal) Babylonian

What a difference between the God of the Christian and the god of Masonry! What an insult to our holy God to be worshiped with the other gods of the ancient pagan nations.

Israel was guilty of this very same abomination. Idolatry was a constant problem with the chosen nation and it was constantly attracted to the worship of the local deities. Using objects as pedestals for the invisible God received severe condemnation from God through the prophets, and provoked God's anger to the point of allowing the Jews to fall prey to their enemies. But it seemed that nothing could stay that Jewish nation from its precipitate departure to disaster.

Solomon introduced a number of foreign deities through the marriages of his many wives and allowed their worship along with Jehovah. The Bible speaks very clearly: this was *evil* in the sight of God. When King Josiah turned to the *true* God, he led the people into a renewal of the covenant with God and this required a reform. He cast out the various cults of Jerusalem, destroyed the vessels that were made for *Baal* which were in the temple, and tore down the "high places" (II Kings 23:8-25). Scripture says there was no king before or after Josiah that turned to the Lord with all his heart, soul and might.

Never is it stated in Masonry that Jesus Christ is God. This is one of the fundamental beliefs of Christianity. Yet the Christian in Freemasonry, upon initiation, receives this charge:

> The world's Great Architect is our *Supreme Grand Master;* and the unerring rule He has given us, is that by which we work. Religious disputes are never suffered within the Lodge; for, as Freemasons, we worship God as our consciences require, and thus we are united in one sacred band.[17]

Here is compromise so subtle that even the Christian fails to recognize it. There is no unity in differing beliefs, "for what fellowship hath righteousness with unrighteousness? and what communion hath light with darkness?" (II Corinthians 6:14) We cannot say that Masonry is compatible with Christianity, for it invites heathen, along with Christians, to its altars.

> Masonry, around whose altars the Christian, the Hebrew, the Moslem, the Brahmin, the followers of Confucius and Zoroaster, can assemble as brethren and unite in prayer to the one God who is above *all* the Baalim, must needs leave it to its initiates to look for the foundation of his faith and hope to the written scriptures of his own religion.[18]

To the unsuspecting Christian, this sounds harmless, even ideal, but is an impossibility. The simple fact remains that the god of the Moslem, the Brahmin or the Confucian is *not* the God of the Christian, the Father of our Lord Jesus Christ. The universal sacred brotherhood of all men, which Masonry insists upon, is erroneous, as is the fatherhood of God. We are all God's offspring by creation because we all come from Adam, but we are not all God's spiritual children. Therefore, it is an impossibility for the Christian to unite in prayer with those

9

who denounce Christ's deity and deny His death on the cross. *For a Christian to stand at an altar believing he is united in prayer with an idol-worshiping pagan suggests one of two things: the Christian is unconvinced of his own message of Good News of what God has done, or he lacks personal conviction that Jesus Christ is the only way to the Father!*

True Christianity refuses compromise with existing religions. Jesus Christ *alone* is the Way to God. Our Gospel requires the declaration of a simple but clear-cut creed: "Jesus is Lord" (Romans 10:9).[19]

Believing in a supreme being is one thing: to know Him through Jesus Christ, our Saviour, is another. Most people start with the notion that there is a God. But this acknowledgement is not enough. The Bible says that "thou doest well" if you believe in one God (James 2:19). But it also says "The devils also believe and tremble." The devils, who will never acknowledge Jesus Christ as Saviour, know there is one God. Agreement that there is one God is not sufficient to save anyone. *God has to be acknowledged in the person of Jesus Christ.* This is the way Thomas acknowledged Him (John 20:28). Acknowledging God through Baal, Mithras, Osiris, Krishna, Allah, Orpheus, Molech, Brahma, Shiva, Vishnu, Zeus, etc., is disgusting and abhorrent to Him. Will the Christian in Masonry be guilty of the same sin the Israelites committed? "For they went and served other gods and worshiped them, *gods whom they knew not;* and *whom He had not given unto them*" (Deut. 29:26). The "brethren" in Freemasonry, by their amiable, discreet and virtuous conduct, are to convince the world of the excellency of their institution. But "that which is highly esteemed amongst men, is abomination in the sight of God" (Luke 16:15).

It is because Masonry maintains that no one has the truth, that all creeds are accepted by the Fraternity.

> Toleration, holding that every other man has the same right to his opinion and faith that we have to ours; and liberality, holding as no human being can with certainty say . . . what is truth, or that *he* is *surely* in possession of it . . .[20]

> No man can say that he hath as sure possession of the truth . . . When men entertain opinions diametrically opposed to each other, and each is honest, who shall decide which hath the Truth; and can either say with certainty that *he* hath it? We know not what *is* truth.[21]

> The cherished dogmas of each of us are not, as we fondly suppose, the pure truth of God . . . Perfect truth is not attainable anywhere.[22]

Masonry poses the age old "question of questions": What is truth? It was Pilate's question, when standing before him was the very embodiment of Truth. Masonry joins Pilate in the implication that there is no absolute truth and suggests that all men have truth who are sincere and honest in their beliefs. Essentially, Masonry teaches, "It doesn't matter what you believe, just as long as you are sincere." What a deadly error this is! A person can be very sincere, but very sincere in the belief of a colossal lie!

While it is correct that most religious creeds have

11

bits and pieces of the truth and have true ideas which bring occasional desirable consequences, Christianity asserts that *all* truth was embodied in Jesus Christ. Scripture declares Him to be full of grace and truth (John 1:4) and Jesus Himself claimed to be "the Way, the *Truth,* and the Life" (John 14:6). If we do not know what is truth, as Masonry claims, then why would the Holy Scriptures teach that we can *reject* the Truth? If we *refuse* to love and welcome the truth, God will send a strong delusion to make us believe what is false (II Thessalonians 2:10-13). Masonry teaches that when men have opinions opposed to one another, no one can determine which one has the truth. Jesus Christ is *not* an opinion. He is God incarnate, "the Way, the Truth, and the Life," and those who know Christ possess truth in its fullest. "And this is life eternal, that they might know thee the only true God, and Jesus Christ, whom thou has sent" (John 17:3).

This tolerant attitude toward another's belief leads directly to the destructive belief that:

> No man has a right in any way to interfere with the religious beliefs of another.[23]

Our assurance that Jesus Christ is the only way for salvation does not, or rather should not, give us the arrogant presumption that we are better than anyone. It should, in fact, create in us a deep joy and love response to tell others of Him. Often this necessitates "interfering" with another's religious beliefs. "Interfering" is not a matter of persecuting or forcing others to believe; it is merely proclaiming

12

a message. If Jesus Christ was just a good man, or Christianity only a body of religious opinions, then there is no message.

The message of the Christian gospel is that salvation is free because of God's incomprehensible love and not because we deserve it. "For by grace are ye saved through faith; and that not of yourselves: it is the gift of God: not of works, lest any man should boast" (Ephesians 2:8-9). All other religious systems are a "do-it-yourself" collection of rules and principles. The Christian proclaims Jesus Christ *alone*. "Neither is there salvation in any other, for there is none other name under heaven given among men whereby we must be saved" (Acts 4:12). Thus, it is *imperative* that we "interfere" to witness and proclaim this glorious message.

This particular teaching of non-interference is in opposition to Christianity. It would mean an end to Christian missions and evangelization, if we were to accept it. Will you, Christian, simply accept Christianity as only a higher species of human faith?[24] Can you recognize continuity or equality between your faith and others?[25] You must not. And yet, this is what Masonry requires!

Biblical Christianity is the truth and can, with certainty, say so — contrary to Masonic teaching. No one but Jesus Christ is Lord and any other means of salvation is futile.

It is clear that the "Supreme Being" Masonry requires belief in, is not the Supreme Being Christianity believes in but can be whatever you conceive him to be.

> To every Mason, there is a God: ONE Supreme, In-
> finite in Goodness, Wisdom, Foresight, Justice, and
> Benevolence: Creator, Disposer, and Preserver of
> all things. How, or by what intermediates He
> creates and acts, and in what way He unfolds and
> manifests Himself, Masonry leaves to creeds and
> Religions to inquire.[26]

Masonic teaching develops a compromising attitude in the minds of its votaries so subtly, that even
some Christians will endorse its teachings. It accepts
all religions and believes that those who follow their
own spiritual paths will attain salvation if they hon-
estly follow such teachings. There is a constant
theme running throughout Masonry of the fusion
and intermingling of all faiths.

> The Kabalistic doctrine . . . like Freemasonry . . .
> incessantly tends towards spiritual perfection, and
> the fusion of the creeds and Nationalities of Man-
> kind.[27]

For the Christian in Masonry, this will
necessitate a compromise of morals and principles.
The end result? Total deception!

> Herein lies the greatest of all deceptions and
> counterfeits — the mingling of true and false reli-
> gion so that all religion is polluted and the purpose
> and plan of the Eternal Creator God, if possible, be
> foiled.[28]

Here are Satan's Masonic religious concepts: all
men believing in *a* Supreme Being can gather
around an altar united in prayer as brothers; no one
knows what is truth; God is the same by whatever
name He is called; no one has the right to interfere

with another's religious beliefs. Can any true Christian adhere to such doctrines?

Masonry has tried to create:

> . . . an atmosphere in which we will never try to convert each other . . . we shall believe in God, avoid criticizing each other, consider all human beings our sisters and brothers, and march forward in a new comradeship of ideas.[29]

Charles W. Ferguson, in his work *Fifty Million Brothers,* has concisely summed up the accomplishment of Masonry:

> Masonry . . . provided a common camping ground for heathen and Christian alike.[30]

*"The Christian message cannot be grafted
upon other beliefs or added to them."* [1]

CHAPTER 2

Occult
and Kabalistic Connections

As stated earlier, Masonry's pretense of honoring the Scriptures is another one of the snares for the Christian. That the Bible is *not* held in higher esteem than any other religious book is a statement which will be hotly disputed by many Christian friends in Masonry. However, Masonic teachings reveal that only in North America is the Bible recognized. Teaching from the "Apprentice" degree discloses:

> The Bible is an indispensable part of the furniture of the *Christian* Lodge, *only* because it is the sacred book of the Christian religion. The Hebrew Pentateuch in a Hebrew Lodge, and the Koran in a Mohammedan one, belong on the Altar; and one of these, and the Square and the Compass, properly understood, are the Great Lights by which a Mason must walk and work. The obligation of the candidate is always taken on the sacred book or books of his religion, that he may deem it more solemn and binding . . .[2]

16

Here is proof that the Bible, which the Christian holds to be *the* written Word of God, is *not* "the only infallible rule for faith and practice." If you were a Hindu candidate for Masonry, you would take your vows on one of their many sacred books, the Vedas, the Brahmanas, or the Upanishads. If you were a Buddhist, you would take your vows on the sacred book entitled The Tripitaka. If Janism were your faith, your vows would be taken on the Agamas. Confucianists would take their vows on the Analects and Five Kings and Taoists would vow on the sacred book of Tao-Teh-King, the Book of Reason and Virtue. Zoroastrianists would prefer the Avestas, Muslims, the Koran. It has been noted in the past that Lodge meetings where numerous religions are present, each place their respective sacred books on the altar, Christians included.

The Living Word (Jesus) and the Written Word (Bible) have always had their rivals in this world, but what an odious, unclean mixture Masonry must be to God! It defies and denies the authority of God's Word, trying to make it equal to other religious writings. Should the Christian in Masonry handle this Book as though it were no different and no more holy than any other book? If he does, then he has caused Christ to be less than He is, because the Living Word and the Written Word are inseparable. Harold Lindsell describes the consequences of defaming either the Living or the Written Word.

There are only two Words of God: the Word of God written, and the Word of God incarnate, Jesus Christ. Both Words are intimately and forever in-

17

terrelated. Whenever one is denigrated or diluted, the other suffers as well.[3]

The Christian believes in the authority of the Bible, the revelation of God to man. We believe in the preeminence of this book above *all* works of mere man. "For the prophecy came not in old time by the will of man: but holy men of God spake as they were moved by the Holy Ghost" (II Peter 1:21). God's Word has no place alongside the pagan babblings of heathenism! In contrast, Masonry accepts all creeds:

> . . . and must needs leave it to its initiates to look for the foundation of his faith and hope to the written scriptures of his own religion.[4]

The above statement, which comes from the degree of "Grand Elect, Perfect, and Sublime Masons," rings with futility and despair because no other written scripture gives a solid foundation of faith and hope, except the Bible. Any Christian believing that the Hindu, Muslim, or Pagan, has *hope* needs to see what God's Word teaches in the book of Romans. *Leading Religions of the World,* by Max Stilson (Zondervan), is a good study of comparative religions which reveals the distinctive message and credentials of Christianity.

There is no hope apart from Jesus Christ; Scripture repeatedly invites men to come to him. No other religious writing offers assurance of justification before God or regeneration in which a person becomes a *new creature here and now*.

Contrary to what the Christians in Masonry have been told, one does not *have* to believe in the authority of the Bible. This is proven by Albert Mackey, one of Masonry's principal writers.

> Although in Christendom very few Masons deny the Divine authority of the Scriptures of the Old and New Testaments, yet to require, as a preliminary to initiation, the declaration of such a belief *is directly in opposition* to the express regulations of the Order.[5]

In fact, teachings from the "Apprentice" degree reveal the Bible, as a Masonic symbol, is unsuitable and inharmonious with other symbols.

> The Holy Scriptures are an entirely modern addition to the symbol . . . Thus the ancient symbol has been denaturalized by incongruous additions . . .[6]

Masons claim that none of their teachings were written down, but are given word-of-mouth. Who would believe such nonsense! Even the Word of God had to be written down so there would be no conflict as to what God required of His people.

It is true that the mystical traditions of Masonry were developed and handed down orally among Jewish Rabbis, but these were finally written down. These writings, known as the Kabalah (Cabala, Cabbala, Cabbalah, Kabala, Kabbala, Kabbalah, Qabbala, Qabbalah) are the source of Masonic teachings and are held in higher esteem than the Bible.

> There are two major books of the Kabbalah, the Sepher Yetzirah, or Book of Formation, and the Zohar or Book of Splendor. The Zohar was written down in Aramaic in Spain around 1275 by a cabalist Moses de Leon.[7]

19

The "brethren" are encouraged to open and familiarize themselves with *these* books — not the Bible.

> Masonry is a search after light, that search leads us directly back to the Kabalah.[8]

> The Kabalistic doctrine . . . like Freemasonry . . . incessantly tends towards spiritual perfection.[9]

> The Source of our knowledge of the Kabalistic doctrine are the books of Jesirah and Sohar.[10]

> The meaning [of the point within a circle] is not for the Apprentice. The adept may find it in the Kabalah.[11]

> This is the doctrine of the Kabalah, with which you will no doubt seek to make yourself acquainted.[12]

The Kabalah, according to the *Sorcerer's Handbook*, is "based on occult interpretations of the Bible."[13] "According to the Cabala, every letter in the Scriptures contains a mystery only to be solved by the initiated."[14] It is considered to be *superior* to the Bible, and cabalists declare that the Bible is incomprehensible without their Cabala! Masonry teaches that the Kabalah is a *second* Bible needed to unveil the symbols and doctrine of the Christian Bible.[15]

The Kabalah teaches that the Bible as a whole is an allegory. Permeated with sexual imagery, the Kabalah contains mystical rites and formulas. It intermingles sorcery and religion, providing the occultist with a great storehouse of magical words and symbols. Cabalists believe the hidden meaning of the Scriptures are unveiled by a specific means, including the manipulation of letters and numbers containing divine powers. The Cabala, comprised of magic, mysticism and supernatural lore, was used for calling upon angels and demons!

The use of numbers and letters is known as *gematria:*

> . . . a system by which Hebrew words converted into numbers and then into other words of the same numbers — and the Names of Powers, the secret names of angels and demons of each sphere which can be used in magical conjuration. Names, like symbols, are believed to possess magical properties . . .[16]

Lewis Spence tells how this manipulation of letters and numbers is done with Scripture.

> Thus the words of several verses in the scripture which are regarded as containing an occult sense, are placed over each other, and the letters are formed into new words by reading them vertically; or the words of the text are arranged in squares in such a manner as to be read vertically or otherwise. Words are joined together and re-divided, and the initial and final letters of certain words are formed into separate words. Again every letter of the word is reduced to its numerical value, and the word is explained by another of the same quantity . . . These permutations and combinations are much older than the *Kabala,* and obtained amongst Jewish occultists from time immemorial.[17]

Medieval magicians used the Kabalistic combinations of the divine names in their rituals.

> The cabbalists attach great importance to the symbolism of letters and numbers, each of which had a particular significance in *divination* and *evocation*

> *. . . Many late magicians and occultists resorted to its words, formulae and symbols (such as the pentagram) as a means of working their magic.*[18]

Any practice of divination, sorcery, or the practice of the magician's art has been strictly forbidden by God. The Word tells us that all who do these things are an abomination to the Lord (Deuteronomy 18:10-14). Seeking supernatural experience apart from the Lord is forbidden; yet this is the purpose of the Kabalah which the "brothers" in Masonry are to acquaint themselves. It was used for divination (foretelling the unknown by occult means), evocation (the calling forth of spirits), and other occult practices.

Is Masonry connected with this abominable system? Yes. It cannot be denied, for the degree of "Knight Kadosh" admits Freemasonry is a child of the Kabalah.

> **Hence Freemasonry, vulgarly imagined to have begun with the Dionysian Architects or the German Stoneworkers, adopted Saint John the Evangelist as one of its patrons, associating with him, in order not to arouse the suspicions of Rome, Saint John the Baptist, and thus covertly proclaiming itself the child of the Kabalah and Essenism together.**[19]

Masonry has always hidden its occult involvement under Christian pretenses, in order not to arouse suspicion. This, too, has been hinted at in the above statement.

In the degree of "Grand Pontiff" it is revealed that the Yezirah and Sohar (which the brethren are to acquaint themselves) "are the completest embodiment of Occultism."[20] Again, in the degree of "Prince Adept" it is declared that the Kabalah:

> taught the doctrine of the Unity of God, the art of knowing and explaining the essence and operations of the Supreme Being, of spiritual powers and natural forces, and of determining their action by symbolic figures; by the arrangement of the alphabet, the combination of numbers, the inversion of letters in writing and the concealed meaning which they claimed to discover therein. *The Kabalah is the key to the occult sciences* . . . [21]

Knowing spiritual powers and determining their action by permutation and symbols is witchcraft! Is this a wild exaggeration? Listen to Masonry's boldest proclamation given in the degree "Master of the Royal Secret."

> The Occult Science of the Ancient Magi was concealed under the shadows of the Ancient Mysteries . . . and is found enveloped in enigmas that seem impenetrable in the Rites of the Highest Masonry.[22]

Is this the Royal Secret? Since Freemasonry has identified itself with the Ancient Mysteries, [see Chapter 1, footnotes 3&4] the occult science concealed under them is now found enveloped in the highest rites of Masonry. What conclusion can we make? None other than the occult science is practiced, but hidden, in the higher degrees of Masonry!

That Masonic symbols come from the Kabalah is proven in the teachings of the degree "Knight of the East and West": ". . . and thus our symbols appear again in the Kabalah.''[23] The degree of ''Prince Adept'' propounds that:

> All truly dogmatic religions have issued from the Kabalah and return to it; everything scientific and grand in religious dreams of all the Illuminati . . . is borrowed from the Kabalah, *all the Masonic associations owe to it their Secrets and their Symbols.*[24]

Masonry depreciates Christianity, stating that Christian teachers are the most ignorant ones of the Bible.

> The Teachers, even of Christianity, are in general the most ignorant of the true meaning of which they teach. There is no book of which so little is known as the Bible. To most who read it, it is as incomprehensible as the Sohar.[25]

In other words, without the Kabalah (those books of mystical letters, symbols, numbers, incantations and formulas) you and I are ignorant of Scriptures. We are ridiculed for our faith in God's Word and are called, in Masonic language, ''the profane.''

Friends in Masonry, Scripture implicitly states, ''. . . no prophecy of the scripture is of any *private* interpretation'' (II Peter 1:20). It also warns that we are not to add to or subtract from the Word. ''Ye shall not add unto the word which I command you, neither shall ye diminish ought from it . . .'' (Deuteronomy 4:2). Masonry, using Kabalistic doctrine and teaching it to its votaries, is offering a cheap counterfeit, and the Christian Mason is being led by seducing spirits. Teachings that weaken the authority of the Scriptures; that distort it; that add to it the thoughts and ideas of man; that deny its divine authority over and above other writings, originate with the god of lies. Scripture tells us exactly who the god of lies is. "Ye are of your father the devil, and the lusts of your father ye will do. He was a murderer from the beginning, and abode not in the truth, because there is no truth in him. When he speaketh a lie, he speaketh of his own: for he is a liar, and the father of it" (John 8:44).

This sinister strategem of using the Bible to gain admiration while secretly using it for occult purposes must be a filthy abomination to God.

The Bible is not esteemed by Freemasonry as Masons are led to believe, but its teachings and symbols come, by their own declaration, from an occult source — the Kabalah. My Christian brethren, the postulant for witchcraft is also given an in-depth study of the Kabalah![26] Let the Christian beware!

*"The affection of possessing a secret is a
childish and mischievous weakness."*[1]

CHAPTER 3

Religious Teachings
of Masonry

Religion, in its narrowest sense, may be defined
as man's search for God. There are many religions
in this world whose paths end in blind alleys.
Masonry is one of them. Most Masons say that the
Lodge does not teach religion, while ignoring the
fact that its buildings are called temples. Yet temples
are buildings for the worship of God or gods. They
also tell me that *if* Lodge teachings are religious,
they are doctrines of the Christian church. We have,
however, already revealed in chapters one and two,
that Masonry identifies itself with the secret worship
rites of pagan gods and proclaims itself a child of the
Kabalah. Because its teachings originate with the
Kabalah, Masonry ignores the central doctrines of
the Christian Church "reducing salvation to mere
moral living without the emphasis on sin and grace,
repentance and forgiveness in Christ."[2]

The fact that Masonry is a religion is maintained
by the Mason's encyclopedist Albert Mackey.

26

> Look at its ancient landmarks, its sublime
> ceremonies, its profound symbols and allegories —
> all inculcating religious observance, and teaching
> religious truth, and who can deny that it is emi-
> nently a religious institution; and on this ground
> mainly, if not alone, should the religious Masons
> defend it.[3]

The degree of "Elu of Fifteen" teaches that
"Masonry is not a religion,"[4] while other degrees
proclaim it to be a religion, even a *worship!*

> Every Masonic Lodge is a temple of religion and its
> teachings are instruction in religion (Royal
> Arch).[5]

> It is the universal, eternal, immutable religion
> (Grand Elect, Perfect and Sublime Mason).[6]

> Masonry propagates no creed except its own most
> simple and Sublime one; that universal religion
> taught by Nature and Reason (Prince Adept).[7]

> That Rite raises a corner of the veil, even in the
> Degree of Apprentice; for it there declares that
> Masonry is a *worship* (Grand Elect, Perfect and
> Sublime Mason).[8]

> Masonry is a worship; but one in which all civilized
> men can unite . . . (Prince of Mercy).[9]

What is this worship, this immutable religion,
which all men can unite in regardless of creed? Is
this religion's doctrine compatible with Christian
doctrine?

The fact that Masonry is identical to the Ancient
Mysteries and its teachings come from the occult
Kabalah should be enough to cause the Christian to

be repulsed by the Lodge. But let us evaluate two important doctrines taught by *true* Masonry which may persuade the Christian Mason to reconsider his vows and support of this deceptive cult.

MASONIC TEACHING CONCERNING SATAN

> The true name of Satan, the Kabalists say, is that of Yahveh reversed; for Satan is not a black god, but the negation of God. The Devil is the personification of Atheism and Idolatry. For the initiates, this is not a *Person*, but a *Force*, created for good, but which *may* serve for evil. *It is the instrument of Liberty or Free Will.* They represent this Force, which presides over the physical generation under the mythological and horned form of the God PAN; thence came the he-goat of the Sabbat, brother of the Ancient Serpent, and the Light-bearer or Phosphor, of which the poets have made the false Lucifer of the legend (The Master).[10]

> The ROYAL SECRET, of which you are a Prince . . . is that which the Sohar [a chief Kabalistic book] terms *The Mystery of the BALANCE.* It is the Secret of the UNIVERSAL EQUILIBRIUM: — Of that Equilibrium between Good and Evil, and Light and Darkness in the world, which assures us that all is the work of the Infinite Wisdom and of an Infinite Love; and that there is no rebellious demon of Evil, or Principle of Darkness co-existent and in eternal controversy with God . . . [Sublime Prince of the Royal Secret].[11]

There are three points here which warrant our attention. First, Masonry teaches that Satan is not a person, but a force. Secondly, it teaches that Satan, this force, presides over all nature under the horned god Pan. And thirdly, there is no rebellious spirit of evil that is in continual opposition to God.

Christianity, in direct opposition to the above statements, *does* believe that Satan, although not a flesh and blood "person," has a definite personality, and is not a mere force. Christianity *does* believe that there is a rebellious devil in controversy with God. The Biblical picture of Satan certainly presents him as a "person" if we apply Trueblood's definition of a person to Satan.

> . . . a being with conscious intelligence, equally able to be conscious of self and of others, and also able both to entertain purposes and appreciate values.[12]

The New Testament is full of allusions to the personality and agency of the Evil One as an adversary of the Kingdom of Grace which Christ came to establish. A created being, he most definitely had a free will, became apostate, and fell from heaven (Luke 10:18). Since that time he has been a bitter enemy against God, but will ultimately be cast into everlasting punishment (Matthew 25:41,46; Revelation 20:10). Christianity teaches that Satan presides over the kingdom of darkness. This kingdom is hostile to Christ's kingdom, the kingdom of light. Satan bears the title of tempter (I Thessalonians 3:5), Beelzebub and prince of the devils (Matthew 12:24), prince of the world (John 12:31; 14:30), god of this world (II Corinthians 4:4), dragon and serpent (Revelation 12:9). Satan's chief characteristics are power and craft. He is known as the strong man

(Matthew 12:29), and a murderer and a liar (John 8:44). Chapter three of Genesis reveals his subtlety and cunning which is exhibited in a delusive trick of transforming himself into an angel of light (II Corinthians 11:14). He was unmistakably *real* in his temptations of Christ, for he spoke to the Lord Jesus, who also spoke to him (Matthew 24). There is only one way from his kingdom of darkness to Christ's kingdom of light — conversion (Colossians 1:13). He is now relentlessly sowing seeds of confusion, doubt and error into the church (Matthew 13:39).

These are the doctrines of Christianity concerning Satan. Not a mere force, he is an intelligent and responsible creature who drags mankind into bondage. Masonry definitely follows Kabalistic teaching regarding Satan. Teachings from the degree of "Grand Pontiff" reveal:

> **LUCIFER, the *Light-bearer!* Lucifer, the Son of the Morning! Strange and mysterious name to give to the Spirit of Darkness! Is it *he* who bears the *Light,* and with its splendors intolerable blinds feeble, sensual, or selfish Souls? Doubt it not!**[13]

Nowhere in Christian doctrine is Lucifer recognized as the one who bears light to the minds and souls of men! It was he who introduced the knowledge of evil to mankind, arguing that man's knowledge of both good and evil would make him an immortal god. Since that day in the Garden of Eden, he has been parading as "light," but only to deceive and bring darkness, despair and suffering to the creation God loves most — man. The immediate consequences of the "light" Lucifer brought to man as a serpent were separation from God and enslavement to himself.

In many pagan religions the serpent was worshiped as the one who brought knowledge (light) to mankind. Often God and Satan are reversed. In the reversed roles we find God as the villain because He wanted to keep Adam and Eve in the dark; He didn't want them to be "wise." The serpent becomes the emancipator because it was through him they gained knowledge which was otherwise hidden. Throughout the Mystery religions, worship of the sun as deity and worship of Lucifer as the giver of light became synonymous.

> . . . the dragon, or Teitan or Satan, became the supreme object of worship, the Titania, or rites of Teitan, occupying a prominent place in the Egyptian Mysteries and also those of Greece.[14]

> "These heretics," says Tertullian, "magnify the serpent to such a degree as to prefer him even to Christ Himself; for he, say they, gave us the first knowledge of good and evil."

> These wicked heretics avowedly worshiped the old serpent or Satan, as the grand benefactor of mankind, for revealing to them the knowledge of good and evil. But this doctrine they had just brought along with them from the Pagan world, from which they had come, or from the Mysteries, as they came to be received and celebrated in Rome.[15]

Both Lethbridge and Hislop agree on the point that the sun and Lucifer were worshiped as one because they both were considered givers of light.

> In Pergamos, and in all Asia Minor, from which directly Rome derived its knowledge of the Mysteries, the case was the same. According to the fundamental doctrine of the Mysteries, as brought from Pergamos to Rome, the sun was the only god.[16]

> Lucifer was the bringer of light. Everyone of course knew that the light came from the sun and so the sun and Lucifer became synonymous.[17]

> From all this, the inference is unavoidable that Satan, in his own proper name, *must* have been the great god of their secret and mysterious worship, and this accounts for the extraordinary mystery observed on the subject.[18]

Be reminded, once again, that Masonry identifies itself with these Ancient Mysteries, presenting "but an imperfect image of their brilliancy."[19]

The problem with the knowledge given by the "light-bearer" was that it was gravely disappointing. With Satan's "light" came immense darkness. Satan decided that man should know both good and evil and know how to mingle the two. To this very day, this notion of the harmony of good and evil is interlaced in the counterfeit religious teachings of the Kabalah, which Masonry employs, and in spiritism, which is dedicated to the union of opposites.

The Bible emphatically states that "God is light and in him there is no darkness at all" (I John 1:4). Jesus, who was God incarnate, said, "I am the Way, the Truth and the Life" (John 14:6). Jesus is the true light-bearer. "In Him was Life and the *life* was the *Light* of men" (John 1:4). *Never*, in Masonry, is Jesus claimed to be the light.

We have established the fact that to the initiate in Masonry, Satan is a force. What else does Masonry teach about this force?

> There is in nature one most potent force, by means whereof a single man, who could possess himself of it, and should know how to direct it, could revolutionize and change the face of the world. This force was known to the ancients. This agent, partially revealed by the blind guesses of the disciples of Mesmer, is precisely what the Adepts of the Middle Ages called the elementary matter of the great work. The Gnostics held that it composed the igneous body of the Holy Spirit; and it was adored in the secret rites of the Sabbat or the Temple, under the hieroglyphic figure of Baphomet or the hermaphroditic goat of Mendes. It is the body of the Holy Spirit, the universal Agent, the Serpent devouring his own tail.[20]

Who is this force, that, if directed even by one man, can revolutionize this world? Masonry has already named him — Satan (see footnote ten of this chapter). Does the horned god Pan, the he-goat of the Sabbat, the hermaphroditic Goat of Mendes and the figure of Baphomet all represent the same thing — Satan?

The horned god was a primitive symbol of power and divinity. Arthur Lyons states in his work *The Second Coming:*

> Wherever the Christian missionaries turned, they found the peasantry worshiping horned gods of fertility. The horned god was spread over the entire Continent, and it was he who was to resist the oncoming Christian tide, becoming miraculously

transformed, for his effort, into Satan, the ruler of
earth in all its glory.[21]

According to Thomas Bulfinch:

> Pan came to be considered a symbol of the universe
> and a personification of nature, and later still to be
> regarded as a representative of all the gods of hea-
> thenism.[22]

He was a Greek deity represented with long pointed
ears, short horns, a man's body and legs of a goat.
Another name for Pan was Capricornus or "the
goat-horned."[23]

It is a well known fact among investigators of
witch cults that the Sabbats include a ritual of
allegiance to Lucifer. It is alleged that the devil appears as a black goat or horned being at these Sabbats. These festivals were remnants of fertility
celebrations in which actors appeared in the guise of
the horned god. The horned god of the Sabbat most
often took the form of a he-goat. Florimond de Re-
mond, councillor of the Bordeaux Parliment in the
seventeenth century, attended a Sabbat and relates in
his *Antipapesse* that on the Eve of St. John sixty per-
sons gathered around a he-goat who was the devil.[24]

Thus far we find a common factor between Pan
and the horned god of the Sabbat: they were both
goat-like. We find also that Baphomet was:

> The goat idol of the Templars (q.v.) and the deity of
> the sorcerer's Sabbath.[25]

What about Mendes?

> The ram or Goat of Mendes represented all of nature as did Pan. This sacred goat was worshiped as a God of fecundity, and all Graeco-Roman sources agree in describing Mendes as a he-goat.[26]

The magician Eliphas Levi, in his famous painting, identifies the Sabbatic goat and the hermaphroditic Goat of Mendes as one and the same.

> The appearance of a goat ascribed to Satan at the Sabbath is an evident survival of antiquity. It is the Mendes of the Egyptian decadence, a combination faun, satyr, and goat Pan, tending to become a definite synthesis of the anti-divinity.[27]

Why have we taken the time to describe all four of these goats? Simply to show that the personal identity of the "potent force" mentioned in Masonry, worshiped in secret rites of the Sabbat, as Baphomet or the Goat of Mendes, can be none other than Satan, Lucifer or the devil of witchcraft. It is the deity of the sorcerer's Sabbat that is the force Masonry claims can revolutionize the world! Sorcery is a form of witchcraft and its god is Lucifer!

It is not unique that Satan would disguise himself as Pan, the god of nature, and representative as all the gods of heathenism. From time immemorial he has directed man's attention from the Lord God of creation to the worship of nature itself. Chapter one of Romans tells of the moral decadence of the people who follow this path.

Christian friend, the potent force of Masonry is none other than the Prince of Darkness. The strange words of our Lord found in the twenty-fifth chapter of Matthew don't appear so strange after all.

> When the Son of man shall come in his glory, and all the holy angels with him then shall he sit upon the throne of his glory: And before him shall be gathered all nations: and he shall separate them one from another, as a shepherd divideth his sheep from the goats: And he shall set the sheep on his right hand, but the goats on the left. Then shall the King say unto them on his right hand. Come, ye blessed of my Father, inherit the kingdom prepared for you from the foundation of the world: Then shall he say also unto them on the left hand, Depart from me, ye cursed, into everlasting fire, prepared for the devil and his angels: And these shall go away into everlasting punishment.

Christ knew all about the horned god, the he-goat, that represented the infernal powers. The first century was a time when witchcraft flourished. That great temple of Diana at Ephesus was none other than a witch cult with Diana as the Great Mother Goddess.

One more word about the he-goat. Occultists today still use, as part of their ritual paraphernalia, a goat's head superimposed within an inverted pentagram. This symbol represents Satan or Lucifer.

MASONIC TEACHING
CONCERNING JESUS CHRIST

In seeking to offend no one, the discussion of religious beliefs is strictly forbidden within the Masonic temple.

> No one Mason has the right to measure for another, within the walls of a Masonic Temple, the degree of veneration which he shall feel for any Reformer, or the Founder of any Religion.[28]

Strange law for a temple of supposedly "Christian" teachings whose God is reported by Christians to be Christ! This tactic, of course, clears the path for Masonry to teach its own mish-mash of Christian and Kabbalistic doctrine without any rebuttal from its initiates. It also closes the door for any Christian Mason to witness for Jesus Christ, or point other masons to saving faith through His shed blood.

The problem lies, as we have already seen, in the fact that Masonry's God is not necessarily Jesus Christ, but can be anything one conceives him to be. This Masonic concept is "deism" which is a "non-specific belief about who God is, a generalized view of Deity."[29] One must simply use the terms God, Great Moral Governor, Grand Architect, Grand Warden of Heaven, Absolute, Legislator, or some vague name when referring to the Deity to avoid breeding division among the brethren.

> Here, as in all the Degrees, you meet with the emblems and the names of Deity, the true knowledge of whose character and attributes it has ever been the chief object of Masonry to perpetuate. To appreciate His infinite greatness and goodness, to rely implicitly upon His providence, to revere and venerate Him as the Supreme Architect, Creator, Legislator of the universe, is the first of Masonic duties.[30]

A paradox (one of many) exists in Masonry. It is always seeking to acquaint its votaries with the true

37

names of the Deity. These names included titles applied to "gods" of all ages from Osiris to Grand Master, but nowhere is the LORD JESUS CHRIST worshiped. There seems to be an actual avoidance of His holy name. L. James Rongstad indicates:

> It is our claim that to avoid the revealed scriptural names for God is a deliberate attempt to deceive by reducing Christianity to just another of the religions of the world. What is even worse, it is succeeding. By doing this, the Lodge effectively de-emphasizes the person and work of Jesus Christ.[31]

I am in complete agreement with Mr. Rongstad. I myself have read the eight hundred sixty-one pages of *Morals and Dogma* and never once found the name Jesus Christ applied to the Deity. However, I discovered that Masonry considers Christ to be nothing more than a teacher of morality and reformer whose teachings were a bit nobler than other reformers.

> None can deny that Christ taught a lofty morality.[32]

> If every man were a perfect imitator of the Great, Wise, Good Teacher, Divine or human, inspired or only a reforming Essene, it must be agreed that His teachings are far nobler . . . than those of Socrates, Plato, Seneca, or Mohamet, or any other of the great moralists and Reformers of the world.[33]

> . . . every true Knight of the Rose Croix will revere the memory of Him who taught it, and look indulgently even on those who assign to Him a character far above his own conception or belief, even to the extent of deeming Him Divine.[34]

> It [Masonry] reverences all the great reformers. It sees in Moses, the Lawgiver of the Jews, in Confucius and Zoroaster, in Jesus of Nazareth, and in the Arabian Iconoclast, Great Teachers of Morality, and Eminent Reformers, if no more: and allows every brother of the Order to assign to each such higher and even Divine Character as his Creed and Truth require.[35]

These four excerpts leave an "open-ended" belief as to the identity of Christ. Essentially Masonry says, "If you want to deem Jesus of Nazareth divine and wish to worship him, that's fine. If you believe Zoroaster was divine, that's fine too. Whomever you deem divine and worship is your business. As for Masonry, we believe they're all great moralists."

Will the Christian in Masonry accept this? I am assuming he understands Christian doctrine concerning the person and identity of Christ.. *God* incarnate. To be wrong on the identity of Christ is eternally fatal.

Masonry, as revealed in the "Knight Rose Croix" degree, believes that Jesus was crucified because of his elevated morality. In contrast, the Bible teaches that He laid down His life willingly to atone for the sin of mankind.

> Whatever higher attributes the Founder of the Christian Faith may, in our belief, have had or not have had, none can deny that He taught and practiced a pure and elevated morality even at the risk and to the ultimate loss of His life.[36]

Everything about Christianity is determined by

the person and work of Jesus Christ. Christ's atoning death is the central theme of both the Old and
New Testaments. Christian doctrine has already determined that he triumphed over the kingdom of
darkness. *He* is the means by which God accomplished his great plan of redemption. But listen to the
teachings of the "Knight Rose Croix" and "Prince
of Mercy" degrees.

> It is not within the providence of Masonry to deter-
> mine how the ultimate triumph of Light and Truth
> and Good, over Darkness and Error and Evil, is to
> be achieved: nor whether the Redeemer, looked and
> longed for by all nations, hath appeared in Judea,
> or is yet to come.[37]

> God is infinitely wise, just, and good . . . at the ap-
> pointed time, He will redeem and regenerate the
> world and the Principle, the Power, and the ex-
> istence of Evil will then cease; that this will be
> brought about by such a means and instruments as
> He chooses to employ; whether by the merits of a
> Redeemer that has already appeared, or a Messiah
> that is yet awaited for, by an incarnation of
> Himself, or by an inspired prophet, it does not
> belong to us as Masons to decide.[38]

Christian friend, will you include yourself in this
belief? Have you not already decided how God has
redeemed the World and through whom redemption
was accomplished? Have you not already met the
Messiah, the incarnate God? If you are going to
adhere to the Masonic order, it will necessitate the
releasing of your beliefs and assuming a position of
uncertainty.

These quotes, again, reveal that Masonry is no more than an "open-ended" religion which embraces all creeds — pagan as well as Christian. A paraphrased version of the above statement could be:

> We Masons aren't really sure and can't really say how God will redeem the world. Maybe He already has, maybe he hasn't. Maybe the instrument He'll choose will be by a redeemer that has already come, or it will be by a messiah yet to come. Maybe redemption will be through an incarnation of himself or perhaps by an inspired prophet. We Masons really can't decide.

Can you not see how a religion such as this attracts all religions to its altars? This is *syncretism*, the adoption of portions of many belief systems. It will destroy the Christian's testimony and power to accept such drivel. We as Christians send the proclamation forth: we have found the Messiah, the Redeemer, the Saviour of all men: Jesus Christ.

We have barely scratched the surface of this deceptive organization called Masonry. The more we study it, the more annoyed we must become with its pretenses. There is gross error in these doctrines, and step by unconscious step, the initiate in Masonry is led down a fraudulent path.

> It is a fact widely ignored, though never without danger, that error rarely appears for what it really is. It is by mingling with or attaching itself to truth that it gains acceptance.[39]

Masonry is more than a social club, school of geometry, or an humanitarian fellowship. It is a religious movement whose god is not the God of the Christian. *It is a "bloodless religion,"* attacking the deity of Christ and denying the superiority of the Scriptures.

We urge all Christians in Masonry to determine for themselves whether these doctrines be of God or Satan. And may you be reminded that involvement in religious error can open the door for demon activity in your life.

*"Baalism and life in Jesus Christ
have nothing to do with one another.
It is time to put away our idols and
follow after the Master."*[1]

CHAPTER 4

Deceptive Symbols

Nowhere in Masonry is the "brother" more cleverly deceived than in the presentation of its varied and ancient symbols. Most symbols are dualistic in nature and Masonic symbols are no exception. Behind all Masonic symbolism there is an undisclosed occult interpretation of which most Freemasons are ignorant.

We already know that Masonry's symbols originate from an occult source — the Kabalah. Kabalistic symbols are employed in the "old religion" (witchcraft) and are avenues by which Satan receives worship for himself. The Blue Lodge Masons are given a supposedly "Christian" interpretation of these Kabalistic symbols. However, it appears that the Blue Lodge is nothing but a deliberate hoax to deceive. That it is a pious fraud is an undeniable assertion made in the degree "Knight Kadosh."

The Blue Degrees are but the outer court or portico

43

of the Temple. Part of the symbols are displayed there to the Initiate, but he is intentionally misled by false interpretations. It is not intended that he shall understand them. Their true explication is reserved for the Adepts, the Princes of Masonry. It is well enough for the mass of those called Masons, to imagine that all is contained in the Blue Degrees; and whoso attempts to undeceive them will labor in vain . . .[2]

Here is deception readily admitted! It appears there is a pseudo-Masonry taught to the majority of Masons and the true meanings of its emblems have been masked, even to its own initiates. Once we trace their origins and meanings, however, we will realize why they have been kept hidden and secret.

We have already educed that Masonry is a sequel to the Ancient Mysteries which was a gigantic system of moral corruption and idolatry.

Their primary objective was to introduce privately, by little and little, under the seal of secrecy and the sanction of an oath, what it would not have been safe all at once and openly to propound.[3]

These Mystery Religions posed a great threat to early Christianity.

Great was the conflict between Christianity and the Mysteries. They did have in common certain aspirations and certain practices; the quest for redemption from mortality and evil . . . certain concepts could easily be refashioned and accepted to Christian belief and practice. But there were some respects in which those who came to Christianity from the Mysteries threatened to subvert the faith.[4]

It is unbelievable that this gigantic idolatrous

44

system is still in existence today under various names and that Christians are ignorantly participating in its pagan rituals. Satan is always trying to foil God's plan by mingling truth with error. He has established alongside the church, with her sanction, a system of idolatry equal to that which plagued ancient Israel in and near Palestine. That system of idolatry is Freemasonry.

Under fair but false pretenses, this organization leads men away from the truth as revealed in Jesus Christ. Were it not for the power of Almighty God, it would be the undoing of the Christian faith. The iniquitous Mystery Religions secretly introduced one corruption after another which were never openly revealed. It would not have been wise or prudent to do so, because the true Chruch may have arrested its progress. Masonry, persisting in this apostasy, has secrets that it cannot openly reveal, for to do so would cause the whole system to sink into overwhelming ruin. It is dangerous for professing Christians to uphold pagan idolatry and yet, *Masonry,* which is *paganism in disguise,* has actually prospered in the bosom of the Christian Church! This truth must be exposed.

The origins of the Mystery Religions are traced to nature worship and vegetation magic. They were generally celebrated with the fall and spring equinoxes. When pagans began to take notice of the annual changes in the earth, they attributed these changes to the dying and reviving of gods and goddesses. Degenerate men then began to worship God through the medium of his creation in the mistaken certainty that through nature's wonders they gained knowledge of the Lord. This, of course, led to idolatry. Believing that they could actually commune with God through nature, they began worshiping the heavenly bodies: sun, moon, stars, nature and the universe. They even regarded the sun as the visible image of God! The gods of the Mystery rites represented the yearly decay and revival of life, especially vegetation life. Nature became the whole manifestation of divinity. In essence, men worshiped immutable objects. Masonry's worship is identical to this idolatry.

> We worship Immutability. It was that steadfast immutable character of the Sun that the men of Baalbec worshiped. His light-giving and life-giving powers were secondary attributes . . . It was not strange that men worshiped the sun.[5]

Masonry, paralleling the pagan worshipers, finds its knowledge of God in nature.

> Nature is the great Teacher of man; for it is the revelation of God.[6]

> All religious expression is symbolism; and the true objects of religion are the SEEN.[7]

> It is true that in one sense, we can have no actual knowledge of the Absolute Itself, the *very* Deity.[8]

> Hence the name of the Deity, taught the ancient Mason, and teaches us, that the true knowledge of God, of His nature and His attributes, is written by Him upon the leaves of the great Book of Universal Nature. This knowledge of God, so written there, and of which Masonry has in all ages been the interpreter, is the *Master Mason's Word.*[9]

> The Unseen cannot hold a higher place in our affections than the Seen and the Familiar.[10]

To the Ancients, God became known as a "Creative Principle" or a "Generative Principle" — the pro-creative or reproductive power of nature. Observing that reproduction came through sex agencies, these Mystery Religions degenerated into orgiastic nature worship and fertility cults. Out of this depravation came phallic cults venerating the reproductive parts of male and female as religious symbols.

> These two Divinities, the Active and the Passive Principles of the Universe, were commonly symbolized by the generative parts of man and woman; to which, in remote ages, no idea of indecency was attached; the *Phallus* and *Ctesis*, emblems of generation and production, and which, as such appeared in the Mysteries. The Indian Lingam was the union of both, as were the boat and the mast and the point within the circle . . .[11]

One of the first symbols presented to the Entered Apprentice Mason is this one of antiquity which is derived from ancient sun worshipers — the point within a circle. The Apprentice Mason, on entering the Lodge, is given a supposedly "Christian" interpretation of this vulgar symbol. He is told that the point is God in the center of the universe, the circle. Or, the point is representative of the individual brother and the circle is his boundary line of conduct. Never is he told that the point actually represents a phallic god, the male generative principle,

47

the impregnating, fructifying force of nature. Nevertheless, all Masonic authorities agree on the derivation of this symbol. This will, no doubt, appear incredible and disputable. But let us examine the writings of two very notable Masons — Prince Adept Albert Pike and Past Grand Master Albert Mackey.

The *Encyclopedia of Freemasonry,* written by Albert Mackey, reveals:

> The phallus was a sculptured representation of the male organ of generation and the worship of it is said to have originated in Egypt. In the Mysteries it was carried in solemn procession . . . And here I think we find the remote origin of the point within a circle, an ancient symbol which was first adopted by the old sun worshipers . . . and incorporated into the symbolism of Freemasonry.[12]

Reading again from this same Masonic source:

> . . . we may collect from the true history of its connection with the phallus of the Ancient Mysteries. The phallus and the point within the circle come from the same source. The first outline of the point within the circle comes from circular temples, or stone circles, with a vast stone in the midst of the circles.[13]

Mackey repeatedly states that the point within the circle is undoubtedly of phallic origin and the point in the circle represents the union of the Ctesis (vagina) and the phallus (penis). In *The Manual of the Lodge* Mackey states:

> The point within a circle is an interesting and important symbol in Freemasonry, but it has been debased in the interpretation of it in the modern

lectures that the sooner that interpretation is forgotten by the Masonic student, the better will it be. The symbol is really a beautiful but somewhat abstruse allusion to the old sun-worship, and introduces us for the first time to that modification of it, known among the ancients as the worship of the phallus.[14]

From Mackey's *Symbolism in Freemasonry:*

Phallus representation of the virile member (male sex organ) was venerated as a religious symbol, very universally by the ancients. It was one of the modifications of sun-worship, and was a symbol of the fecundating (impregnating) power of that luminary.[15]

The Phallus was in imitation of the male generative organ. It was represented usually by a column which was surmounted by a circle at its base, intended by the ancients as a type of the prolific powers of nature which they worshiped under the united form of the active or male principle and the passive or female principle.[16]

The point within the circle is derived from sun-worship, and is in reality of phallic origin.[17]

Albert Pike states:

It is but an old term revived. Our adversaries, numberable and formidable as they are, will say and will have a right to say that our Creative Principle is *identical* with the Generative Principle of the Indian and Egyptian, and may fitly be symbolized as it was symbolized anciently by the linga (penis). To accept this in lieu of a personal God is to abandon Christianity and the worship of Jehovah, and to return to wallow in the styes of Paganism.[18]

Let us reiterate a moment. Pike says that the Creative Principle of Freemasonry is the same as the Generative Principle of India and Egypt — the linga. Mackey states that the linga (male sex organ) is the point in the circle which comes from ancient sun-worship. The Apprentice is told that the point (the veiled linga) is God in the center of the universe.

How clearly we see who the God of Freemasonry really is — none other than Lucifer himself. It certainly isn't the God of the Christian who receives worship through the genitals! Do we now see why Masonry's Creative Principle, its god, is called ''The Great Architect of the Universe'' (G.A.T.U.)?

A Kabalistic figure, the point within the circle, is a disguised form of veneration of the male and female sex organs taken from phallic cults of antiquity. The ''Prince of the Tabernacle'' degree encourages the Mason to penetrate the meanings of this emblem.

> The Christian Fathers contented themselves with reviling and ridiculing the use of these emblems. But as they in earlier times created no indecent ideas, and were worn alike by the most innocent youths and virtuous women, it will be far wiser for us to seek to penetrate their meaning. Not only the Egyptians . . . but every other people that consecrate this symbol (the Phallus), deem that they thereby do honor to the Active Force of the universal generation of all living things.[19]

Another symbol associated with the point within the circle is the Hebrew letter YŌD.

> In the East of the Lodge, over the Master, inclosed

in a triangle, is the Hebrew letter YŌD. In the English and American Lodges the Letter G is substituted for this as the initial of the word GOD, with as little reason as if the letter D, initial of DIEU, were used in French Lodges instead of the proper letter. YŌD is, in the Kabalah, the symbol of Unity, of the Supreme Deity . . . It must suffice to say, that it is the Creative Energy of the Deity, is represented as a *point,* and that point is the centre of the *Circle* of immensity. It is to us in this Degree, the symbol of that unmanifested Deity, the Absolute, who has no name.[20]

The letter "G" which is placed over the Master of the Lodge is really a substitute for the Hebrew letter YŌD which is the Kabalistic symbol for the "Creative Energy" represented by the point. That point, which we have already discovered, is the male sex organ in disguise. The tragedy of the whole thing is that the Christian Mason believes that the letter "G" stands for his God through Jesus Christ, or geometry, which is a subject lectured on in some degrees. But the "Prince Adept" degree is very clear as to what this "G" or YŌD represents.

Adam is the human Tetragram, which is summed up in the mysterious YŌD of the Kabalah, image of the Kabalistic Phallus.[21]

With what does Masonry substitute the phallus? An obelisk.

Death is the inseparable antecedent of life; the seed dies in order to produce the plant, and earth itself is rent asunder and dies at the birth of Dionysos. Hence the significancy of the *phallus,* or of its

> inoffensive substitute, the obelisk, rising as an
> emblem of resurrection . . . [22]

The obelisk, disguising the phallus, is the Mason's symbol of resurrection. It is interesting to note that obelisks often serve as monuments of famous men who have been Masons. One good example of this is the Washington monument. Washington was a Mason. Since he was a fasting and praying Christian, he must have been deceived by the chicanery of the Masonic organization as are millions of others.

The blazing star is yet another deceitful symbol employed in Freemasonry which is said to be an emblem of Divine Providence. We can turn once again to the Ancient Mysteries to find the real meaning of this symbol.

> To find in the BLAZING STAR of five points an allusion to the Divine Providence is also fanciful; and to make it commemorative of the Star that is said to have guided the Magi, is to give it a meaning comparatively modern. Originally it represented SIRIUS, or the Dogstar, the forerunner of the inundation of the Nile; the God ANNUBIS, companion of ISIS in her search for the body of OSIRIS, her brother and husband. Then it became the image of HORUS, the son of OSIRIS, himself symbolized also by the Sun . . . It was HERMES, also . . . It became the sacred and potent sign or character of the Magi, the PENTALPHA . . . [23]

Tracing the five pointed star from its modern meaning back to its origins in Egypt, we find that it is actually the pentagram or pentalpha, the sign which summarizes all the occult forces of nature. According to the *Sorcerer's Handbook*:

> The domination of the mind over the elements, and the demons of the air, the spirits of fire, the phantoms of

52

water and ghosts of earth are enchained in this sign.[24]

The Pentagram, which in Gnostic schools is called
the Blazing Star . . . the Star of the Magi . . . and
according to the direction of its points, this absolute
magical symbol represents order or confusion, the
Divine Lamb of Ormus and St. John, or the accurs-
ed goat of Mendes. The Pentagram with the two
points in the ascendent represents Satan as the goat
of the Sabbath; when one point is in the ascendent,
it is the sign of the Saviour.[25]

All mysteries of Magic, all symbols of Gnosis, all
figures of occultism, all kabalistic keys of prophecy
are summed up in the Sign of the Pentagram.[26]

This geometric Pentagram, which represents the
mysteries of deity and creation is held to be the most
powerful means of conjuration in any rite.

This symbol has been used by all secret and occult
societies, by the Rosicrucians, the Illuminati, down
to the Freemasons today.[27]

Because the occult science was concealed under
the Ancient Mysteries and is now found enveloped
in the rites of highest Masonry, we can come to only
one conclusion. The occult star that Masonry
employs is the Kabalistic symbol of the Microcosm.
Using this pentagram in various positions evokes the
powers of light and darkness according to William
Singleton, 33[0]:

This star represents God, all that is pure, virtuous and
good when represented with one point upward; but
when turned with one point down it represents EVIL,
all that is opposed to the good, pure and virtuous; in
FINE it represents the GOAT of MENDES.[28]

53

For those who would argue about the Masonic star, it would be well to remember that all Masonic symbols come from the Kabalah; the Kabalah is the key to the occult sciences; all postulants for witchcraft are given an in-depth study of it.

> The cabbalists attached great importance to the symbolism of letters and numbers, each of which had a significance in divination and evocation . . . Many later magicians and occultists resorted to its words, formulas and symbols (such as the pentagram) as a means of working their magic.[29]

In the occult, a star with one point up represents white magic and two points up represents black magic. Any magic, whether "white" or black, "good" or evil, is worked out by the powers of Satan. The Christian is forbidden by God to use any magical art of any sort. (Deuteronomy 18:9-14) The Israelites were commanded of God not to learn the abominations of the pagan nations surrounding them and these abominations included all the magical arts — witchcraft, sorcery, necromancy, spiritualism, astrology, divining, false prophecy, spells, omens, etc. Participation in any false religious cult, Masonry included, opens up doors for fellowship with demons.

As previously stated, all Masonic symbols are symbols of ancient idolatrous religious ceremonies. The *lamb's skin apron* originates with the religious initiations in the worship of various sun gods.

> In Crete, Jupiter, Ammon, or the Sun in Aries . . . the same as Osiris, Adoni, Adonis, and

other Sun-Gods — had also a tomb, and a religious initiation; one of the principal ceremonies of which consisted in clothing the Initiate with the skin of a white lamb. And in this we see the origin of the apron of white sheep skin used in Masonry.[30]

The two-sided Mason's square:

> . . . is a very ancient glyph reading "Builder" and apparently was first used in crosses symbolizing the Sacred Four . . . [31]

> The two-sided square is a symbol which is constantly found in the Book of the Dead, also in various papyrii. All seats where either gods or goddesses are shown sitting are composed of the two-sided square. In the Great Hall of Truth where Osiris is shown sitting in judgment, his seat is composed of the two-sided square.[32]

> The Square indicates the religion of Nature.[33]

The dagger of the degree "Elu of Nine," with its black blade and white hilt, emblem of the two principles of Light and Darkness, represents the dagger used in the Mysteries of Mithras.[34] The ring in the fourteenth degree comes from the Gothic Mysteries of Anubis. The sprig of acacia (evergreen) which is thrown into the grave of a deceased Mason orginates with the legend and worship of Osiris.

One could go on at length discussing Masonic symbols, but detailed interpretation of them would take much time. We do know, without a doubt, that Masonry freely admits to lying and deception concerning its symbols.

> Masonry . . . conceals its secrets from all except Adepts and Sages, or the Elect, and uses false ex-

planations and interpretations of its symbols to mislead those who deserve only to be misled; to conceal the Truth, which it calls Light, from them and to draw them away from it.[35]

The question arises: Who *are* the Adepts, Sages and Elect? *Those who practice the occult sciences.* Masonry's astrological emphasis, Kabalistic doctrine, identity with the Ancient Mysteries, occult symbols, numerology and alchemic instruction, seal its doom with God and His people.

Magism is definitely emphasized in Pike's Morals and Dogma.

> To this science [occult], said the crowd, nothing is impossible; it commands the elements . . . and can bestow on its adepts riches by the transmutation of metals, and immortality by its quintessence and elixir compounded of gold and light. This is what magic had been . . . when positive Christianity . . . publicly crushed this philosophy with its anathemas, and compelled it to become more occult and more mysterious than ever. Christianity should not have hated magic; but human ignorance always fears the unknown.[36]

> The dunces who led primitive Christianity astray, by substituting faith for science . . . have succeeded in shrouding in darkness the ancient discoveries of the human mind.[37]

> The Kabalah is the primitive tradition, and its entirety rests on the single dogma of Magism . . .[38]

> Another Jewel is necessary for you . . .It is what is termed the Kabalistic pantacle [five pointed or six pointed star] . . . This carries with it the power of commanding the spirits of the elements. *It is nec-*

essary for you to know how to use it, and that you will learn by perseverence if you are a lover of the science of our predecessors the Sages.[39]

The Jewel for the Mason of the Prince Adept degree is the occult pentagram which is used in *witchcraft* and other occult sciences for conjuration rites!

The truth has been revealed here in this chapter as to the nature and origins of Masonic symbols. It is clear to us now why Albert Pike stated that the Bible is a modern addition completely incongruous with the other Masonic symbols. What blasphemy to add God's Word as a symbol to these vulgar symbols used in pagan worship rites.

It is hoped, Christian reader, that these few symbols which have been exposed in this chapter will convince you of this gigantic Masonic web of deception. If you have been entangled in it will you not sever yourself from this vast idolatrous system? Repent and return to a pure, unadulterated faith in Jesus Christ.

*"Too many of us have been playing carelessly
with vows which are more potent than
dynamite in their power to scar our immortal souls."*[1]

CHAPTER 5

Self-Destructive Oaths

Masonry's boast of having its origins with the building of King Solomon's temple is more bait for the believer. Indeed Solomon's magnificent temple must have been rather spectacular, but one can hardly understand the fascination and preoccupation with it found in Freemasonry. Using the temple as the greatest representation of the builder's art, it allegorically links the physical temple to a spiritual temple, "a house not made with hands, eternal in the heavens." Solomon's temple becomes the spiritual home of every Mason, a prototype of the spiritual temple in the human soul.

> We were but as apprentices bound to learn the craft. **Example.** The free mason setteth his apprentice first a long time to learn to hew stones, and when he can do that perfectly, he admitteth him to be a free mason and chooseth him as a cunning man to be a master of the craft, and maketh him a setter or orderer of the same stone . . . And so to build to

Almighty God a glorious and pleasant temple in our souls, we as the workmen, and He as the principal author and master of the work. Now in diverse degrees, according to their exercise in grace, every person buildeth in his soul a temple to God, some more some less, as the clearness of their consciences requireth . . .[2]

As he pursues light (not the light of the Gospel), the Mason is supposedly given lessons in the use of the working tools of the stone craftsman so that eventually he is portraying the master architect of King Solomon's temple, Hiram. Now why a Christian would want to portray Hiram is an unanswerable question. In its feeble attempts to establish a "kinship" between present stone masons and the builders of Solomon's temple, Masonry has fabricated a legend about Hiram so absurd it gains admirability just for its folly! Interpreting the account of the building of the temple given in the third and fourth chapters of II Chronicles as symbolic of man's struggle for perfection, Masonry again tries to hide its true identity under Biblical pretenses. It guides the Christian toward a whited sepulcher.

Masonic authorities agree that Masonry was *not* founded at the building of King Solomon's temple, but thousands of years before in Egypt.

The story that the fraternity was founded at the building of King Solomon's temple, has enjoyed uninterrupted existence ever since, is one of the *myths* of the organization which has been innocently believed by many, but which does not merit serious attention.[3]

> Legendary Masonry goes back to the building of King Solomon's temple when Hiram Abiff, a Mason, is said to have chosen death rather than reveal the secret Masonic word. *No serious historian attaches any credence to the legend.*[4]

> It is admitted that the secret system of Freemasonry was originally founded on the Mysteries of the Egyptian Isis, the goddess-mother, or wife of Osiris.[5]

How many Christians have swallowed the myth that Freemasonry began at the building of King Solomon's temple? In reality, it succeeds the pagan Mystery Religions, and acts as a rival to Christianity.

The worship of resurrected gods characterized these Mystery Religions. By the time the message of a resurrected Christ was being proclaimed to the Gentile nations, many resurrected gods and goddesses were being worshiped. The heathen attempted to add Jesus Christ to the list of deities. It was in this way that the Mysteries became a threat to Christianity.

While there were many who opposed the iniquitous system of these Mysteries, there were others, who, while professing the Christian faith, brought along their predilection for pagan feasts and rituals. They tried to amalgamate paganism and Christianity. Satan skillfully grafted the celebration of Christ upon similar celebrations of dead and risen gods in the Mysteries, and a thin cloak of Christianity was thrown over pagan customs. There has been formed what Alexander Hislop termed *"Christianized pa-*

ganism," which has produced tremendous rivalry to true Christianity.

Patterned after these ancient Mysteries, Masonry, the largest and most ancient secret order in existence, carries on this tradition of rivalry. It competes with the Church in its expansive system of benevolence.

> Masonry teaches man to practice charity and benevolence, to protect chastity, to respect the ties of blood and friendship, to adopt the principles and revere the ordinances of religion, to assist the feeble, guide the blind, raise up the downtrodden, shelter the orphan, guard the altar, support the Government, inculcate morality, promote learning, love man, fear God, implore His mercy and hope for happiness.[6]

These are indeed admirable goals which appear to be Christian. But we have already discovered many glaring inconsistencies, and all that appears to be Christian in Masonry is canceled out by the pervading influence of pagan religions. It is *impossible* to reconcile Masonry to Christianity. Perhaps the greatest hindrances to this reconciliation are the barbaric oaths Masonry requires of its candidates under threat of the most hideous penalties. These oaths in which the "brother" offers his body for mutilation are murderous and vile.

The candidate for Masonry enters the Lodge by way of secret initiation rites and vows which are very similar to those of the Mysteries. What the unsuspecting candidate doesn't know is that he is actually being initiated into the religion of Isis. How many

Masons know that the initiation rites into a witch coven also originate from the same source as Masonry's? The Ancient Mystery Religions are the vile source of both.

> One fascinating ritual practiced by the Egyptians is initiation into the Mystery Religion . . . (many contemporary witches trace their own initiation rituals back to these complicated rites).[7]

The fact that Masonry and witchcraft have similar origins should not surprise us. We have already seen, in previous chapters, that they serve the same god — Lucifer!

Initiation into the first Masonic degree, Entered Apprentice, is accomplished in a ceremony known as the "Shock of Entrance." After numerous instructions and being divested of his clothing, the candidate clothes himself in garments supplied by the Lodge, but is told to leave his left breast bare. Following a series of questions which he must answer, he is escorted by the Senior Deacon to the altar. The Deacon removes the compass from the altar, presses the point to the candidate's naked left breast and states:

> Mr. _____ , on entering the Lodge for the first time, I receive you on the point of a sharp instrument pressing your naked left breast, which is to teach you, as this is an instrument of torture to your flesh, so should the recollection of it ever be to your mind and conscience should you attempt to reveal the secrets of Masonry unlawfully.[8]

Thus fear is instilled in the "brother" at the outset

and the cherished compass is to be recollected as an instrument of torture!

Perle Epstein tells of the test of fear which the witch candidate must pass which is strikingly similar to that of the Apprentice Mason.

> **Each novice enters alone after passing the test of fear (a knife point placed symbolically at his breast) and is bound hand and foot.**[9]

After meeting the officers of the Lodge, the Apprentice then prepares to take his solemn obligation while kneeling, resting his hand on the Bible, square and compass (that instrument of torture). The oath consists of promises never to reveal the secrets of the craft by any means — speaking, writing, stamping, cutting, carving or engraving — and ends with the following penalty:

> **. . . binding myself under no less penalty than that of having my throat cut from ear to ear, my tongue torn out by its roots and buried in the rough sands of the sea at low-water mark where the tide ebbs and flows twice in twenty-four hours, should I ever knowingly or willingly violate this my solemn oath and obligation as an Entered Apprentice Mason. So help me God, and keep me steadfast in the due performance of the same.**[10]

This oath and other Masonic "secrets" are available to anyone willing to seek the truth. Even a small town library will yield quite a bit of information. However, I came across a Masonic ritual book written in code which contained all the initiation rites for the first three degrees. Entitled *King Solomon and His Followers,* its code appeared as follows:

> . . . bndg msl und n ls pn thn tt % havg m th ct fm e t e,
> my tg tn ou b its rts @ bd in H sns % t c at l wt mk . . .[11]

One can see that the code is quite simple and by replacing vowels and consonants, the oath is revealed. The oaths and rituals for each degree were written in the same manner. For each succeeding degree the penalty that accompanies the oath becomes more atrocious. The penalty for the second degree, Fellow Craft, is as follows:

> . . . binding myself under no less penalty than having my left breast torn open, my heart plucked out, and given as a prey to the wild beasts of the field and the fowls of the air.[12]

The penalty for the Master Mason's oath is:

> . . . having my body severed in twain, my bowels taken from thence and burned to ashes, the ashes scattered to the four winds of heaven, so that no more trace or remembrance may be had of so vile and perjured wretch as I.[13]

Each of these oaths conclude with the phrase "so help me God."

It is astounding that a Christian could call upon God to act as a witness in the taking of these oaths. To what wickedness has he bound himself? Just this — he is giving this group of men permission to murder for the protection of a secret. And by enjoining himself to the Lodge by these vows, *he* has the right to execute (*it will be his obligation to execute*) the penalties on others, should they betray the brotherhood. Everyone under these oaths becomes a would-be assassin and has entered into a criminal bond. The Holy Spirit-guided Christian would certainly shrink from such obligations.

> It should wound the sensibilities of the faithful Christian to call upon God to the accompaniment of hideous penalties to help him preserve the trivial secrets of Masonry.[14]

Masons entering the Ancient Arabic Order of Nobles of the Mystic Shrine, otherwise known as the "Shriners," are required to take their vows on the faith of a Moslem. The incredible truth is that many ministers have taken this Shriner's oath:

> . . . on my voluntary desire, uninfluenced and of free accord do hereby assume, without reserve, the Obligations of the Nobility of the Mystic Shrine, as did the elect of the Temple of Mecca, the Moslem and the Mohammedan. I do hereby, upon the Bible, and on the mysterious legend of the Koran, and its dedication to the Mohammedan faith, promise and swear and vow on the faith and honor of an upright man, come weal or woe, adversity or success, that I will never reveal any secret part or portion whatsoever of the ceremonies I have already received . . .[15]

This is a lengthy oath which also carries a ghastly penalty:

> In willful violation whereof may I incur the fearful penalty of having my eyeballs pierced to the center with a three-edged blade, my feet flayed and I be forced to walk the hot sands upon the sterile shores of the Red Sea until the flaming sun shall strike me with a livid plague, and may Allah, the god of Arab

Moslem, and *Mohammedan, the god of our fathers,* support me to the entire fulfillment of the same. Amen. Amen. Amen.[16]

Can the Christian glibly state that Mohammedan is the "god of our fathers?" Should he call upon Allah, god of the lost Moslem?

At one time in the history of our nation, May 1833, fourteen hundred citizens petitioned the United States Congress to prohibit, by law, the Masonic oaths. The committee from the House of Representatives recommended that the oaths be legally prohibited on the grounds that they were not lawfully authorized; they bind a person to violate the law; they were subversive and blasphemous; their penalties were forbidden by the U.S. Constitution.[17]

Masonry holds its oaths as irrevocable even though a member withdraws from the Lodge, is expelled or suspended. The oaths bind one in chains of fear which only Christ can break. I talked with a gentleman who had demitted from the Lodge 30 years ago who was still under its bondage. This was quite evident when I asked him if I could use some of his Masonic material for this manuscript. His fear of letting the "secrets" be known surfaced at that point. To be free from this bondage of fear, the Christian must confess and repent of his sin of taking the oath and renounce, in the name of Jesus, his involvement in this occult organization. It is important to hear the Word of the Lord concerning the taking of oaths.

And Moses spake unto the heads of the tribes con-

cerning the children of Israel, saying, This is the thing which the Lord hath commanded. If a man vow a vow unto the Lord, or swear an oath to bind his soul with a bond; he shall not break his word, he shall do according to all that proceedeth out of his mouth (Numbers 30:1-2).

When thou shalt vow a vow unto the Lord thy God, thou shalt not slack to pay it; for the Lord thy God will surely require it of thee; and it would be sin in thee. That which is gone out of thy lips thou shalt keep and perform; even a freewill offering, according as thou hast vowed unto the Lord thy God, which thou hast promised with thy mouth (Deuteronomy 24:21,23).

Or if a soul swear, pronouncing with his lips to do evil, or to do good, whatsoever it be that a man shall pronounce with an oath, and it be hid from him; when he knoweth of it, then he shall be guilty in one of these. And it shall be, when he shall be guilty in one of these things, that he shall confess that he hath sinned in that thing (Leviticus 5:4-5).

Who can deny that a Christian has pronounced with his lips to do evil on the swearing of the Masonic oaths? These Old Testament injunctions may seem ancient and out-of-date, but they are confirmed by the word of our Lord in Matthew 12:34-37.

O generation of vipers, how can ye, being evil, speak good things? for out of the abundance of the heart the mouth speaketh. A good man out of the good treasure of the heart bringeth forth good things: and an evil man out of the evil treasure bringeth forth evil things. But I say unto you, That every idle word that men shall speak, they shall give account thereof in the day of judgement. For by thy words thou shalt be condemned.

Is the Christian pronouncing "words of life" in the taking of his vows?

Clearly, *Lodge oaths are contrary to God's Word.* The foregoing is adequate to show the sin of the Christian in taking these oaths — the sin of offering one's body for mutilation.

With its braggadocio of building "to Almighty God a glorious and pleasant temple in our souls," Masonry requires the Christian who takes his vows to deliver his own body, *which is the temple* of the Holy Spirit, for destruction. Hear the Word of the Lord.

> And what concord hath Christ with Belial? or what part hath he that believeth with an infidel? And what agreement hath the temple of God with idols? for *ye are the temple of the living God;* as God hath said, I will dwell in them, and walk in them; and I will be their God, and they shall be my people (II Corinthians 6:15-16).

> What? Know ye not that your body is the temple of the Holy Ghost which is in you, which ye have of God, and ye are not your own? For ye are bought with a price: therefore glorify God in your body, and in your spirit which are God's (I Corinthians 6:19-20).

Your body, Christian, is the temple of God, purchased by the precious blood of Christ. To agree to the mischief of Masonic vows which would destroy it is sin. Jesus Christ is the *only* one who can negate the obligation of your vows, but it will require confession and repentance.

Masonry cannot be reconciled to Christianity because of its vows. But there is also, in the Mason's Eucharist, teachings that are completely anti-Christian. If they were the only evidence we had that this organization is blasphemous, it would be all we would need.

The lesson of the Scottish Trinitarian degree (Prince of Mercy) is a series of questions put forth by the Senior Warden. After questioning the Junior Warden on the nine great Truths of the Sacred Mysteries, the Senior then asks:

What is to us the chief symbol of man's ultimate redemption and regeneration?[18]

To which the Junior Warden replies:

The fraternal supper, of bread which nourishes, and of wine which refreshes and exhilarates, symbolical of the time which is to come, when all mankind shall be one great harmonious brotherhood; and teaching us these great lessons: that as matter changes ever, but no single atom is annihilated, it is not rational to suppose that the far nobler soul does not continue to exist beyond the grave: *that the many thousands who have died before us might claim to be joint owners with ourselves of the particles that compose our mortal bodies;* for matter ever forms new combinations; and the bodies of the ancient dead, the patriarchs before and since the flood, the kings and common people of all ages, resolved into their constituent elements, are carried upon the wind over all continents, *and continually enter into and form part of the habitations of new souls* . . . And thus, in the bread we eat, and in the wine we drink tonight, *may* enter into and form part of us the iden-

tical particles of matter that once formed parts of the material bodies called Moses, Confucius, Plato, Socrates, or Jesus of Nazareth. In the truest sense, we eat and drink the bodies of the dead; and cannot say that there is a single atom of our blood or body, the ownership of which some other soul might not dispute with us . . . To our Jewish Brethren, this supper is symbolical of the Passover: to the Christian Mason, of that eaten by Christ and His Disciples when celebrating the Passover . . .[19]

We see presented here three views of the communion meal: the Mason's (which is clearly *not* the Christian's), the Jewish and the Christian's.

When we Christians share in the Lord's table we witness to the Gospel. We take the elements of bread and wine as signs and seals of Christ's last will and testament. We are saying that our salvation is dependent upon His sacrifice on the cross. We attest to the fact that we are in touch with a living Christ. And even though Christ said to "eat the flesh of the Son of man, and drink his blood," he did not mean that we would actually eat and drink the material particles of his body (as Masonry decrees), but that we would live in a spiritual sense. However, only those who have received a spiritual new life in Christ can understand His words. The natural man, who cannot understand spiritual things, will make the Eucharist something other than what it is. We are indeed in union with Christ, but not because we've literally eaten matter that once formed the material part of His body. Receiving Christ as Saviour is feeding upon Spiritual Bread. Christ is the "food" of *spiritual* life. The Lord's table is a perpetual reminder of how God-in-Christ gave himself to us eternally.

It is important to keep in mind that it is the *Lord's* table. Masonry makes a mockery of this for it also becomes the table of Moses, Confucius, Plato, Socrates and anyone else's whose body particles happen to have been "carried upon the wind" and are in the bread we eat and the wine we drink. From this, Masonry claims new bonds of sympathy and brotherhood between each man because he has, "in the truest sense," eaten and drunk the bodies of the dead. Furthermore, Masonry decrees that the many thousands who have died before us might claim to be joint owners with ourselves. This is the "great lesson" Masonry teaches about the bread and wine.

Jesus Christ did not command his disciples to eat the communion meal in remembrance of the thousands who have died before. He said, "Do this in remembrance of *me.*" The fraternal supper of Masonry profanes the Holy Communion and defies the Lord's command. The Christian who participates in this meal within the Lodge is a partaker of the sins of blasphemers. We are to remember Him and only Him. It is Jesus Christ and only He who brings life and light to men's hearts. Neither Moses, Confucius, Plato or Socrates can illumine men's minds with truth, for Christ alone is Truth.

> Jesus commands us to do this in remembrance of him; but we would do it without the command because we seek, in every way at our disposal, to remember him who is the way, the truth and the life.[20]

71

One cannot consistently subscribe to the teachings of both the Masonic Lodge and Christianity. Dr. A.J. Gordon of Boston says this about assimilating ourselves with secularism:

> We become unavoidably and insensibly assimilated to that which most completely absorbs our time and attention.[21]

Dr. James M. Gray, former president of Moody Bible Institute gave this caution:

> One cannot be constantly mixed in secular society without unknowingly losing some of his interest in the divine society of God and of angels, where he belongs by his new birth. Our citizenship is in heaven, my Christian brothers, and we ought to be careful where we are living and refuse to be attracted by any system which is a rival of the blood-bought church of the Redeemer.[22]

Christian, I urge you to break the yoke that binds you by your secret oaths, through confession and repentence. Jesus Christ wants your total allegiance. You cannot serve two masters. Refuse from this moment forward to be attracted by this system of rivalry which demands you to "halt between two opinions."

> Prove your loyalty by refusing to have any traffic with an organization which stifles your Christian confessions, dims the light of the eternal truth you have received from Holy Scripture, and compromises your Christian way of life to the point of making it indistinguishable from the way of the world.[23]

*"Whoever calls any man "Grand Master"
makes himself a grand slave. Let everyone who
enters a secret society know that he parts with
his liberty, puts his neck under a yoke,
and fetters his feet . : ."*

CHAPTER 6

Come Out and Be Separate

One of the things our natures fight against so
stubbornly is being wrong. All of us are, to some degree or another, untrue to our holy God. Sometimes
we are unconscious of our sinful nature and practices which we have hidden even from our own flesh
(Isaiah 58:7). Because we cannot see our own blind
spots, sins, and wrong doing the Lord wills that we
might be subject one to another and receive one
another's rebukes and reproofs. By using members
of the Body of Christ, God has created a system of
checks and balances within the Church. But we
detest it! When someone has reproved us in the
Spirit of Christ and has pointed out some error in
our lives, we become "ruffled" and would rather die
than admit our wrongs. The truth is that we cannot
grow spiritually if we do not confess our sins. But if
we admit our errors, which requires a death to self
and ego, there is a life-giving change which brings
unspeakable joy. The Lord Jesus Christ often re-

veals our hidden darkness or ignorance by the Holy Spirit through His Word or another member of the Body. Then there is for the Christian only one course of action: to admit our wrong, confess, repent, and renounce the sin.

Most of us do not want to hear negatives. We close our ears to them and choose not to believe them. Why? It may be that we will have to change our way of thinking, repent and have our walls of pride and self-righteousness torn down. What we fail to see is that *the revelation of negatives clears the way for the positive power of the cross* in our lives.

Without a doubt this small volume is a compilation of negatives about the Masonic Lodge, but only so that the deception which mars the whole structure might be revealed. God is in the process of exposing all deception. Everything — every person, organization, and structure — will eventually stand naked before God. "For there is nothing hid, which shall not be manifested; neither was anything kept secret, but that it should come abroad" (Mark 4:22). "Fear them not therefore: for there is nothing covered, that shall not be revealed; and hid, that shall not be known" (Matthew 10:26). It is hoped that this work will aid the "undressing" process so that Christians can clearly see that the undergarments of Masonry are "filthy rags."

This book is an injunction to those who express a loyalty to Jesus Christ not to do so with lying lips. It is a call to Christians to do what thousands of other Christians were led to do — come out and be separate. It is a charge to our brothers and sisters in

Christ who have enjoined themselves to the Lodge to admit their wrong, for an unwillingness to confess sin is an indication of self-righteousness. Scripture admonishes, "And have no fellowship with the unfruitful works of darkness, but rather reprove them" (Ephesians 5:11). This is a reproof of the works of darkness. Christian, will you hear it?

Many testimonies have been given against secret orders and lodges. Great leaders of the past, and many contemporary laymen have risked the loss of friends, jobs and security to denounce the Lodge. One of these was a man by the name of Stephen Merrit, a Mason, and Master of the biggest lodge in New York. Here is his testimony.

> About a month ago there was a precious meeting in the Tabernacle with our poor people. There came a great hush upon the congregation. The Holy Spirit was there in power, as we talked of Him. It was a solemn time. I felt subdued and close to God and said, "I am Thine: I am altogether Thine, Lord." But the Holy Ghost said, "THAT WEDGE OF GOLD!" I said, "All is thine. There is nothing between me and Thee." He only said, "THAT WEDGE OF GOLD!" Then I remembered under the floor of my tent, oh, I had hidden a wedge of gold! I had kept a beautiful jewel which was a present from the lodge and worth $250 or more, made of gold, with a diamond suspended in it.

> I wrote a letter to the Temple Lodge No. 203, and told them God had told me to sever all connection with Masonry forever. Then I enclosed the jewel and sent it. The members of the lodge came to talk with me. I was told it would ruin my business; that it would hurt me in a thousand ways. "Don't

break off,'' they pleaded. They wanted me to keep the jewel. They said, ''We don't know what to do with it.'' I told them I would not give it houseroom. They might melt it up and give it to the poor, if they wanted to. It was a wedge of gold in my tent and I would have it there no longer.

That was only about a month ago. It was the last link that bound me to the world. Now I am free. I will not have anything between Jesus and my soul. In this convention I am standing for the first time a free man! For whom the Son makes free, he is free indeed. I never had such blessed deliverance.

I thank God the seal of the Spirit is on me; that I am walking in the light. They used to lead me about blindfolded in the lodge. It was the blind leading the blind into the ditch. We must get out of that mire, and put our feet on the solid foundation, the Rock Christ Jesus. There only are we safe.[2]

Stephen Merritt relates another experience he had as a member of the lodge that should be a warning to others.

But I found the tendency of the whole thing evil, and only evil, continually. So I protested and left, but still paid dues and attended funerals. I was a very dull scholar.

One incident helped to open my eyes. I have always preached that there is no other name but Christ by which we can be saved. But again and again I found Masons dying without God and without hope. I was called to the bedside of one member of my lodge who was thought to be dying. He gave me the grip as I sat down by him. He said he was dying and was in great distress for his soul. I tried to have him look to Christ. But he reproached me, saying I had led him astray. I had told him in the lodge, as Master, that a moral life was enough. He said, "You told me then that it was all right if I was an upright man, and obeyed the precepts of the lodge, but I am leaning on a broken reed; and now I am dying without God. I lay this to your charge, Worshipful Master. I leaned on you and now I am dying."

I groaned in agony and fell on my knees and cried to God to spare the man's life. My heart was almost broken. God heard and spared the man, but he has since died a Christian. He was converted, and told me I must get out of the lodge; that I could not be consistent as a Christian and a Mason. But I did not see it. Ministers and other good men are in the lodge. They help to make it a delusion and a snare. The times of such ignorance God winked at, but now every man is commanded to repent of lodge folly.[3]

Dwight L. Moody, famous evangelist and founder of Moody Church in Chicago, had this to say about secret organizations:

I do not see how any Christian, most of all a Christian minister, can go into these secret lodges with unbelievers. They say they can have more influence for good; but I say they can have more influence for good by staying out of them, and then reproving their evil deeds. You can never reform anything by unequally yoking yourself with ungodly men. True reformers separate themselves from the world. "But," you say, "you had one of them in your church." So I had, but when I found out what it was I cleaned it out like a cage of unclean birds. [Here Moody was referring to a secret temperance union.] "But Mr. Moody," some say, "if you talk

77

that way you will drive all the members of secret societies out of your meetings and out of your churches." But what if I did? Better men will take their places. Give them the truth anyway, and if they would rather leave their churches than their lodges, the sooner they get out of the churches the better. I would rather have ten members who are separated from the world than a thousand such members. Come out from the lodge. *Better one with God, than a thousand without Him.* We must walk with God, and if only one or two go with us, it is all right. Do not let down the standard to suit men who love their secret lodges or have some darling sin they will not give up.[4]

I appeal to the reader, if he or she belongs to a secret lodge, to let the scales fall from your blind eyes. Then walk out into the sunlight of freedom and forgiveness by repenting of lodge folly, as did Stephen Merritt. Ignorance, which God may have winked at, can no longer be an excuse. You can no longer say, "I didn't know." Now you know. *Masonry and Christianity contradict one another.*

It has been indisputably shown, from Masonic sources, (principally Albert Pike and Albert Mackey, both of whose writings are found in every American Lodge and regarded as standard works by all American Masons) that Freemasonry, in America, just as in Europe, is a religious sect diametrically opposed to Christianity. It has its own altars, temples, priesthood, worships, ritual, ceremonies, festivals, consecrations, anointings, its own creed, its own morality, its own theory of the human soul and the relation of that soul to the deity, and attempts to displace Christianity. Its "G.O.D." is merely a symbol for nature . . . Its "Bible" is not

78

the Christian Book of Divine Revelation (which is held to be an imperfect form of the Jewish Kabbala), but is merely *one* of many religious books, such as the Koran, the Vedas, the Zenda-vesta, the Book of Mormon, etc. The morality of the Mason is pagan sensuousness; its much-vaunted benevolence is devoid of the charity of Christ.[5]

At a session of the Synod of the Reformed Presbyterian Church in Philadelphia, June 1894, the following statement was adopted concerning secret societies:

Such a society is contrary to the spirit and letter of the religion of Jesus Christ. The grip, the password, the darkened window, the guarded door are not Christlike, and the Christian, especially the minister of Christ, is out of place in such surroundings.[6]

And here are the words of Leo XIII:

Freemasonry, under the pretense of vindicating the rights of man and reconstituting society, attacks Christianity; denounces the divine Sacraments, and everything sacred as superstition. On its own part it preaches the worship of nature . . . May God in His mercy bring to nought their impious designs; nevertheless, let all Christians know and understand that the shameful yoke of Freemasonry must be shaken off once and for all . . .[7]

This author feels that the real horror of this whole system is that it is helping Christians to do away with Christianity without their being aware of it. Christians, and especially ministers, are helping Masonry to be a delusion and a snare. It is a subtle device for discrediting Christianity, and is responsible for the eternal damnation of many individuals.

The Christian Mason has been confronted with the negatives of Masonry, its contradictions. He has a choice: to retreat into his world of secrecy or admit his error and repent. Admitting wrong is *never* easy. It means dying to ourselves and our "rightness." For the Mason, it means giving up the WEDGE OF GOLD he so proudly wears.

We conclude with this address by former president of Moody Bible Institute, Dr. James M. Gray, urging Christians to come out of the lodges.

> In conclusion, I do not expect that anything I am saying will change the mind of any lodge member, but I sincerely hope to be instrumental under God in saving some young men, and especially students of the Christian ministry, from entanglement with what I consider to be a great delusion; to plead with them to separate themselves from the whole system, as I would plead with them about any other moral or spiritual counterfeit. I plead with them to separate themselves from it, because it is dishonoring to Jesus Christ; because it is hurtful to the truest interests of the soul; *because it has the stamp of the dragon on it.*[8]

> *"Wherefore come out from among them, and*
> *be ye separate, saith the Lord."*

The following is a condensed version of a sermon preached by Dr. Alva J. McClain while he was pastor of the First Brethren Church of Philadelphia, Pennsylvania. Pastor McClain was founder and president of Grace Theological Seminary of Winona Lake, Indiana. Used by permission of BMH Books, Winona Lake, Indiana 46590. The full text of the original message may be obtained in tract form from the publisher.

CHAPTER 7

Freemasonry and Christianity

I have two texts: Matthew 12:30 — "He that is not with me is against me;" John 12:48 — "He that rejecteth me, and receiveth not my words, hath one that judgeth him: the word that I have spoken, the same shall judge him in the last day." Will you listen carefully while I present three propositions? (1) Jesus Christ is God manifest in the flesh; apart from Him the true God can neither be known, worshiped, nor acknowledged. (2) Salvation is by faith in the atoning blood of the Lord Jesus Christ, apart from all human works and character. (3) It is the supreme obligation of every saved person to obey the Lord Jesus Christ in all things.

These three propositions are the pillars of the Christian faith — the deity of Christ, salvation by faith in Him, obedience to His Word. Do you believe these three things?

About four weeks ago I called over the telephone one of the highest officers of the Grand Lodge, at his office at the Masonic Temple in Philadelphia. I told him frankly that I was not a Mason and that I desired to obtain some authentic information regarding Freemasonry and its religious position. This officer suggested three books by Masonic authorities. I told him that one would be sufficient and asked him which of the three books was the best. Without hesitation he answered, "Get the *Encyclopedia of Freemasonry* by Mackey. It is without question, our highest and best authority." He then referred me to a man at the Masonic Library. I called him and asked him for the highest and most authentic Masonic authority. Without a moment's hesitation he answered, "Get the *Encyclopedia of Freemasonry* by Mackey." I have that encyclopedia with me here tonight. In the main, my analysis of Freemasonry will be based upon its statement and claims. Surely, no Mason can question the fairness of this method. My examination of Freemasonry tonight will be absolutely from the viewpoint of a Christian. I have nothing to say to Masons who are not Christians. If I were not a Christian, I would undoubtedly be a Mason tonight, as I was preparing to enter when the Lord Jesus saved my soul. I am speaking to those who own Jesus Christ as Lord and God. I shall not assume to speak for Freemasonry tonight; Freemasonry shall speak for itself. By its own utterances, by its own words, Freemasonry must stand justified, or condemned (Matthew 12:37).

I. MASONRY CLAIMS
TO BE A RELIGIOUS INSTITUTION

This claim is made not once in this encyclopedia, but literally dozens of times in different articles. Under the article on "Religion" Dr. Mackey discusses fully the right of Masonry to be called a "religious institution." Dr. Mackey gives in full Webster's definition of "religion" and proves conclusively that Freemasonry meets every requirement of Webster's three primary definitions of religion, and sums up the proof in the following words:

> Look at its ancient landmarks, its sublime ceremonies, its profound symbols and allegories — all inculcating religious doctrine, commanding religious observance, and teaching religious truth, and who can deny that it is eminently a religious institution . . . ? Masonry then, is indeed a religious institution; and on this ground mainly, if not alone, should the religious Mason defend it.

This should settle for all time the question as to whether or not Freemasonry is a religion. According to its own claims, it is proper to speak of the "religion of Freemasonry." The man who contends that Freemasonry is not a "religious institution" is childishly ignorant of the organization or else he is a willful deceiver!

Now I desire to lay down a Biblical truth. Here it is: There is only ONE true religion. That religion is Christianity. All other religions are false. We are now in a position where we can determine absolutely whether or not the religion of Freemasonry is false or true. Here are the propositions. There is but one true religion — Christianity; Freemasonry has a religion. If it is not Christianity, it is false; if it is Christianity, it is true. The issue is perfectly clear. Freemasonry has answered the question. Mark carefully the answer on page 618 of the encyclopedia: "The religion of Freemasonry is not Christianity!" These are not my words. They are the words of Masonry's encyclopedia, prepared by one of the greatest Masonic authors, recommended to me as authentic by one of the highest officers of the Grand Lodge in Philadelphia! It declares Freemasonry has a religion and that religion is not Christianity! Does any man care to stand up and say that a Christian can belong to and support an institution which teaches a religion which is not Christian? The curse of God is upon every religion outside of Christianity.

II. FREEMASONRY RATES CHRISTIANITY AS A "SECTARIAN RELIGION" WHILE BOASTING OF ITS OWN "UNIVERSALITY."

Again I quote from the encyclopedia:

If Masonry were simply a Christian institution, the Jew and Moslem, the Brahman and the Buddhist, could not conscientiously partake of its illumination; but its universality is its boast. In its language, citizens of every nation may converse; at its altars men of all religions may kneel; to its creed, disciples of every faith may subscribe (p.439).

Can you as a Christian sit unmoved by such a dastardly comparison between Christianity and

Masonry? According to this noted Masonic authority, Christianity is a sectarian religion. Christianity can be compared with Mohammedanism, Buddhism, and Brahmanism. It is the religion of Masonry that belongs down in the market place alongside of Buddhism, Brahmanism, and Mohammedanism! Christianity belongs above them all! Oh you Christians here tonight, is our Christ only a sectarian Christ, deserving only a place alongside of these false prophets? I tell you NO! (Daniel 7:13-14, John 1:29, John 12:32, I John 2:2, Philippians 2:9-11).

III. MASONRY DOES NOT CONFESS JESUS CHRIST AS LORD AND GOD. THEREFORE, THE GOD OF MASONRY IS NOT THE TRUE GOD.

Masonry has a god — you can't have a religion without a god. And this god has a name. Over and over in this encyclopedia you meet with the initials "G.A.O.T.U." This is the god of Masonry. The initials stand for the name "Great Architect of the Universe." This is the god that the Masons worship at their altar. This is the god to whom Mason prayers are offered.

Now I shall present the Christian view of God. Let me sum it up briefly: There is one true God. This true God is revealed in the Person of Jesus Christ. Apart from Christ there is no true God. If a man confesses Jesus Christ, he is confessing the true God. If he worships Jesus Christ, he is worshiping the true God. If a man refuses to confess Jesus

Christ as God, he is denying the true God. If he refuses to worship Jesus Christ, he is refusing to worship the true God. Now we are ready for the question, ''Is the god of Masonry the true God, or is he a false god?''

The answer depends absolutely upon Masonry's attitude toward Jesus Christ! If Masonry asks its initiates to acknowledge and confess Jesus Christ as Lord and the true God, then Masonry's god is the true God. But if Masonry does not require its members to confess and acknowledge Jesus Christ as Lord and the true God, then the god of Masonry is not the true God! But let Masonry speak for itself (p. 619). ''THERE IS NOTHING IN IT (MASONRY) TO OFFEND A JEW!'' Do you know what this means? Let me tell you. The Jews condemned Jesus Christ to death and delivered Him to the Romans for crucifixion because He claimed to be their God. I tell you, if there is nothing in Masonry to offend the Jew, then Masonry does not confess Jesus Christ as Lord and God, nor ask its initiates to do so. And if Masonry does not confess Jesus Christ, then Masonry does not confess the true God. And if Masonry does not confess the true God, then Masonry confesses a false god. And if Masonry confesses a false god, let us be plain and call Masonry what it really is, by its own utterances, in the light of the Bible — nothing but paganism and idolatry! (I John 5:20-21, I Corinthians 6:9-10).

But, someone may say: ''It is true that Jesus Christ is not confessed in the first three degrees, but He is confessed as God in some of the higher degrees of Masonry.''

Suppose I should start an organization here in this church with secret work and several degrees. The first three degrees would eliminate the name of Jesus Christ and demand that every candidate confess a god named "G.A.O.T.U." We would accept Christians, Jews, Mohammedans, Buddhists. After they had passed the first three degrees, we would say: "Now, if you Christians want to get together and confess your Christ, go up in a room by yourselves. You Mohammedans do the same, and so forth. But don't drag your peculiar views into these three degrees." That's what Masonry does. What a pitiful sop to throw to our Blessed Lord Jesus Christ! As a Christian I spurn it. Masonry had better left Him out altogether than to offer Him this crowning insult.

Masonry even goes so far as to mutilate the Word of God in order to exclude Jesus. I have here another work by the author of the encyclopedia. It is called "The Masonic Ritualist." It gives the prayers and Scriptures which are to be read in the opening and closing of the lodge. Every Scripture used is emptied of Jesus Christ, but there is a particularly glaring mutilation on page 271. I shall give the quotation exactly as it appears in the "Ritualist" followed by the author's explanatory note:

CHARGE TO BE READ
AT OPENING THE LODGE

Wherefore brethren, lay aside all malice, and guile, and hypocrisies, and envies, and all evil speakings. If so be ye have tasted that the Lord is gracious, to whom coming as unto a living stone, disallowed indeed of men, but chosen of God, and precious; ye also as living stones, be ye built up a spiritual house, an holy priesthood, to offer up sacrifices acceptable to God . . . (The passage of Scripture here selected is peculiarly appropriate to this degree . . . The passages are taken, with slight but necessary modifications, from the second chapter of the First Epistle of Peter . . .)

You will note that Dr. Mackey says some "slight but necessary modifications" have been made in these Scriptures. What are these modifications? Let me read I Peter 2:5 from the Bible and you will see. "Ye also, as lively stones, are built up a spiritual house, an holy priesthood, to offer up spiritual sacrifices, acceptable to God *by Jesus Christ.*" Do you see it? The name of Christ is struck out by the profane hand of Masonry! There are in the "Masonic Ritualist" 28 prayers, and not one of them is offered in the name of Jesus Christ! Let me read you one passage — I John 4:3 ASV — "Every spirit that confesseth not Jesus Christ is not of God: and this is the spirit of the antichrist, whereof ye have heard that it cometh; and now it is in the world already." These are not my words. These are the words of God. Do you dare, as a Christian, wear the emblem of such an organization?

IV. BEFORE ACCEPTING ANY CHRISTIAN AS A MEMBER, MASONRY DEMANDS THAT HE DISOBEY JESUS CHRIST

Obedience to the Lord Jesus Christ is the first and supreme duty of every Christian (John 14:15, I John 2:3-4). Now let me read something that was commanded by the Lord Jesus in the most solemn manner. "Swear not at all; neither by heaven; for it is God's throne; nor by the earth; for it is his footstool: neither by Jerusalem; for it is the city of the great King" (Matthew 5:34-35). Practically every Mason admits frankly that the taking of oaths is necessary to become a member. On page 522 Dr. Mackey discusses the "obligation of Masonic secrecy." He says the opponents of Masonry have brought five charges against this Masonic obligation of secrecy:

(1) It is an oath.
(2) It is administered before the secrets are communicated.
(3) It is attended by a penalty.
(4) It is accompanied by certain superstitious ceremonies.
(5) It is considered by the Masons as paramount to the obligations of the law of the land.

Mackey says further: ". . . it may be granted, for the sake of argument, that every one of the first four charges is true. The last charge is indignantly denied." But the first four are true! Thus it is that

Masonry with impunity asks men to disobey Jesus Christ, but at the same time it insists sternly that all its own mandates shall be obeyed immediately and implicitly. Page 525 points out:

> The first duty of every Mason is to obey the mandate of the master (not Christ, but the master of the Lodge). The Masonic rule of obedience is like the nautical imperative: "Obey orders, even if you break owners."

Jesus Christ is the Owner of the Christian and the Christian must obey Him, not the profane voice of Masonry.

V. MASONRY TEACHES ITS MEMBERS THEY MAY REACH HEAVEN, LIFE AND IMMORTALITY BY A WAY APART FROM JESUS CHRIST

If the Word of God teaches anything, it teaches that apart from Jesus Christ no man will ever reach heaven, see life, or receive immortality. (John 14:6, I John 5:12). Masonry ignores Jesus Christ as the true Way of salvation. These Masonic books contain not the slightest hint which I can find that any Mason can be lost forever. From this mass of testimony I choose one quotation. Among its other paraphernalia, Masonry has a ladder which is brought into the lodge for the work of initiation. On page 361 this encyclopedia gives the meaning of the ladder.

> This ladder is a symbol of progress . . . its three principal rounds, representing Faith, Hope, and

> Charity, present us with the means of advancing
> from earth to heaven, from death to life — from
> mortal to immortality. Hence, its foot is placed on
> the ground floor of the Lodge, which is typical of
> the world, and its top rests on the covering of the
> Lodge, which is symbolic of heaven.

This is the Masonic way into heaven. The initiate is to climb into heaven by the ladder of Faith, Hope and Charity. Will such faith, hope and charity save the soul of any man? You know it will not. If a man has nothing more than faith in God (and remember that the god of Masonry is not the true God), nothing more than hope for immortality, nothing is more certain than that that man will be lost. There is only one faith that can save — that is faith in the Lord Jesus Christ. The ladder of Masonry is not the Way of Jesus Christ! The entrance to heaven is not by a ladder. It is by a door! (John 10:9)

I can think of only four reasons why you find professing Christians affiliated with the Masonic Lodge:

First — Some do not know what Christianity really is. Many have the prevalent but erroneous opinion that Christianity and religion are one and the same. If an organization is religious and talks about God, they conclude it is Christian.

Second — Some do not know what Masonry really is. You may think that such ignorance is impossible. Not at all! The average Mason is like some church members. He only does what is absolutely necessary to become a member and stops there.

Third — A few professing Christians continue

their relations with Masonry in spite of the fact that they know what Christianity is, and also what Masonry is. Such as these are without excuse. They are living every day in deliberate disloyalty to the Lord Jesus Christ who died for their sins.

Fourth — There are some professing Christians in Masonry who are apostate from the true faith. Some of the preachers in Masonry belong in this classification. They have relegated such truths as blood atonement and the deity of Christ to the place of nonessentials.

I must close, though I have only begun. This encyclopedia contains enough that is anti-Christian to keep me preaching for the next ten weeks every Sunday night. I have tried not to be harsh or unkind. I have tried to tell the truth. "It will hurt me if I leave Masonry now!" I know it will! But, oh Christian, did your Christ fail you at the cross because it hurt? By the blood of the cross I plead with you: "Come out from among them and be ye separate."

Lecture of the 32nd Degree
By James D. Shaw
Former 33rd Degree Mason

Introduction:

Symbolic Blue Lodge Masonry consists of three degrees: the Entered Apprentice, Fellow Craft and Master Mason. All Masons, without exception, must pass through these three degrees before he may seek further light (?) in the various other Rites and Degrees.

"The Entered Apprentice . . . is a preliminary degree, intended to prepare the candidate for the higher and fuller instructions of the succeeding degrees. The Apprentice degree is devoted to the beginner; the Fellow Crafts to a more advanced searcher for light. Master Mason constitutes the Third Degree, and, as practiced today, the last of Blue Lodge Masonry. As we have it today, the Master Mason Degree is actually incomplete, because it needs a complement which is only supplied in the Royal Arch Degree. The symbolism of the Master Degree, as we have it now, is necessarily restricted to the First Temple and to the present life, although it reaches a climax in the assurance of a future life (without the aid of the Bible, God, Jesus Christ, or the church)." (From the Masonic Bible by John A. Hertel Co. pp. 10-11 the parentheses are ours).

After passing through these three degrees of sham Symbolic Blue Lodge Masonry, which Sovereign Grand Commander Albert Pike declares to be a deliberate hoax to deceive the simple candidate into thinking that he knows something of the secrets, when he actually knows nothing at all, he may be enticed to pursue other Rites and Degrees in the institution.

A Jew or other person who is anti-christ in their philosophy would likely find Chapter Masonry unoffensive; since it is thoroughly Jewish in its ritual. If one were inclined towards philosophical Christianity, yet, himself not a true believer in the person of Jesus Christ, he might be inclined toward the Rite of the Templars, for what Albert Pike calls, "A Christian Interpretation of Masonry."

If, however, a man is a run-of-the-mill, get-in-it-for-gain type, as most of them are, he will likely end up in the Scottish Rite. The Masonic Bible says it "Is the most popular and most widely diffused of all the Rites" (Masonic Bible by John A. Hertel Co., p. 14).

Much is said in Masonic literature about the work involved: the meditation, contemplation, diligent labors and searchings of the candidate for the grand

and glorious light, which is supposed to be found in the mysteries of the higher degree. But nothing could be further from the truth! For example: Joseph Smith, founder of the Mormon cult, stated that he received all three degrees of the Blue Lodge in one day! Seeing that both Joseph Smith and Brigham Young and all the other male followers of these two false prophets were made Masons on their way to Utah, just might account for the numerous similarities between the two cults. It might account also for the strong belief among Mormons that Joseph, their prophet, was murdered by Masons. (See Cecil McGavin's book *Mormonism and Masonry*.)

Furthermore, all twenty-nine of the Scottish Rite Degrees may actually be obtained in thirty days or less! James D. Shaw, former 33rd Degree and past Master to all Scottish Rite bodies explains just how this is accomplished:

"Once or twice a year, usually in the spring, all candidates for the Scottish Rite Degrees are rounded up. And after paying a sizeable fee, these people are assembled in some secluded hall or auditorium where they watch a cast act out the ritual of the various degrees. At the end of each of these short presentations, one individual — some prominent citizen — is selected to stand in for all the other candidates present; and by proxy receive the degrees for them. This process goes on for about four sessions covering seven or eight degrees per session. At the conclusion of the final session all candidates have been elevated to the sublime Prince of the Royal Secret (32) Degree. And in reality knows very little, if anything more, of Masonry than he did four weeks earlier! But that is immaterial to the average candidate, for he sees Masonry only as a stepping stone to worldly success.

LECTURE OF THE 32ND DEGREE

Masonic philosophy teaches that the 32nd Degree of Masonry is supposed to make a Mason a better man and a Christian a better Christian. After you have read the lecture of this degree, you decide for yourself if you think it would make you better in any way. The following is the Lecture of the Thirty Second Degree of the Ancient and Accepted Scottish Rite as delivered by James D. Shaw 33 Degree and Past Master to all Scottish Rite bodies:

"We now come to the great symbol of Pythagoras (the Greek philosopher). Our symbols have descended to us from the Aryans, and many were invented by Pythagoras, who studied at Egypt and Babylon. In order to preserve the Great Truths from the profane (anyone not a Mason), there were invented some of our symbols that represent the profoundest of truths descended to us from our white ancestors. Many have been lost. Lost, as was the Great Word at the death of Hiram Abiff.

"The ancient Masons invented some of these symbols to express the results of their contemplation of deity. They did not attempt to name him, but rather tried to express their reverence by describing him as Ahura-Mazda, spirit of light (Ahura Mazda is a nature god of Zoroastrianism, a Persian god worshiped with fire).

"They conceived the idea that Ahura had seven potencies or emanations. Four of these they thought of as being male and three female. The four male potencies of Ahura by which he governed the Universe were: the divine might, the divine wisdom, the divine word and the divine sovereignty. The three female potencies were: productiveness, health and vitality.

"Behold, in the east the seven pointed star, the great symbol of this degree, with the seven colors of the rainbow. The seven colors and the seven points represent the seven potencies of Ahura.

Observe now the great delta of Pythagoras consisting of 36 lights arranged in eight rows, to form an equilateral triangle. The light at the apex of the delta represents Ahura Mazda, source of all light. This represents the seven remaining potencies of Ahura.

The right angle triangle of three lights around the altar represents the famous 47th proposition of Euclid, or the Pythagorian theorem, which is used to conceal and reveal philosophical truths. The real significance of the cross is that of Ahura and his four male emanations, emanating from him. The four animals of the prophet Ezekiel represent these same four male emanations: man, the divine word; the eagle, divine wisdom; the bull, divine might and the lion, divine sovereignty.

"Every equilateral triangle is a symbol of trinity, as are all groups of three in the lodge, in the sacred and mystic symbol "AUM" of the Hindoos, whose origin and meaning no one here knows. The great trinity of the Aryans was symbolized by the Adepts.

Among the Hindoos it symbolized a supreme god of gods. The Brahmins, because of its awful and sacred meaning hesitated to pronounce it aloud. And when doing so placed a hand in front of the mouth to deaden the sound. This triliteral name for god, is composed of three sanskrit letters. The first letter "A" stands for the creator (Brahma); the second letter "U" for (Vishnu) the preserver; the third "M" for (Siva) the destroyer. "AUM," it is eneffable, not because it cannot be pronounced, because it is pronounced A-A-A-U-U-U-M-M-M. All these things which you can learn by study, concentration and contemplation, have come down to us from our ancient ancestors through Zarathustra and Pythagoras.

"You have reached the mountain peak of Masonic instruction, a peak covered by a mist, which you in search for further light can pierce only by your own efforts. Now we hope you will study diligently the lessons of all our degrees, so that there will be nurtured within you a consuming desire to pierce the pure white light of Masonic wisdom.

And before we let you go, let me give you a hint; and that is all that the great mystics ever give, as to how you may learn to find that light. The hint is in the Royal Secret, that true Word. Man is born with a double nature: what we call good and what we call evil; spiritual and earthly; mortal and immortal. And finds the purpose of his being only when these two natures are in perfect harmony, like the harmonies of the Universe. Harmony my brethren, harmony is for the true word and the Royal Secret which makes possible the empire of true Masonic brotherhood.''

Now we ask you: what is there in this lecture that would make even the rankest sinner, much less a born-again Christian, a better person? Absolutely nothing! For this lecture of blasphemy equates the One True and Eternal God of the Bible with the nature gods of the Pythagorian, Zorastrianean and Hindu! It teaches the poor simple Mason the Satanic, pantheistic, theosophical eastern philosophy that he already has within himself the good, spiritual, immortal and divine nature, which is totally anti-Scriptural! He is taught that by harmonizing the mortal fleshly part with the immortal — divine part — within himself, he will find harmony within himself as there is harmony in the Universe. And all this may be accomplished by man himself, without the help of God, the Bible, the Lord Jesus Christ, His blood, or His church!

"Because when they knew and recognized Him as the God, they did not honor and glorify Him as God, or give Him thanks. But instead they became futile and godless in their thinking — with vain imaginings, foolish reasonings and stupid speculations — and their senseless minds were darkened. Claiming to be wise, they became fools — professing to be smart, they made simpletons of themselves.'' (Romans 1:21-22 The Amplified Bible).

Petition For Withdrawal

LODGE #_____

CITY _____

STATE _____

Gentlemen:

When initiated into the Entered Apprentice degree, I was induced to swear that, "I will always hail, ever conceal and never to reveal any of the secret arts, parts or points of the hidden mysteries of ancient Freemasonry, which have been heretofore, may at this time or shall at any future period be communicated to me as such." In my ignorance, and being led along line by line, I indulged in the bloody oath you required of me.

Now, gentlemen, after having examined the highest documents of the institution of Freemasonry, I have found that the god of Masonry is positively not the God of the Bible. Freemasonry has nothing whatsoever to do with the Bible. Freemasonry is in no way compatible with Christianity.

Being a Christian as I am, and confessing the Lordship of Christ, as I do, and having learned of the true nature of the institution of Masonry, I present to you my Petition For Withdrawal.

I renounce my association with, and my obligations to the craft of Masonry, without the least equivocation, mental reservation, or self evasion of mind. For the Word of God explicitly says:

> "Be ye not unequally yoked together with unbelievers; for what fellowship hath righteousness with unrighteousness? And what communion hath light with darkness?"

Please believe me, that I have no animosity toward you gentlemen; or any other man in the Lodge. It was not you that deceived me. It was the institution of Freemasonry that deceived us both.

Respectfully,

Mr._____

Date _____

Footnotes and Bibliography

Chapter 1: Compromise for the Christian

1. Stevens, Albert C., *The Cyclopedia of Fraternities*. New York: E.B. Treat Company, Second Edition, 1907, p. 12.

2. *The Ahimon Rezon*. Philadelphia, Pennsylvania: Williams Brothers Press, 1928, p. 174.

3. Pike, Albert, *Morals and Dogma of the Ancient and Accepted Scottish Rite of Freemasonry*. Richmond, Virginia: L.H. Jenkins Incorporated, 1921, p. 22.

4. *Ibid.*, p. 23.

5. Mackey, Albert G. and Edward L. Hawkins, "Mysteries, Ancient," *An Encyclopedia of Freemasonry*. New York and London: The Masonic History Company, 1920, Vol. II, p. 497.

6. Pike., *Op. cit.*, p. 352.

7. Bainton, Roland H., *The Horizon History of Christianity*. New York: American Heritage Publishing Company, 1964, p. 75.

8. Hislop, Alexander, *The Two Babylons*. Neptune, New Jersey: Loizeaux Brothers, Second American Edition,

1959, p. 12.

9. Mackey, *Op. cit.*, p. 352.

10. Hislop, *Op. cit.*, p. 14.

11. Wilkinson, "Ancient Egyptians," London, 1837-41, quoted in Hislop, Alexander, *The Two Babylons*, 1959, p. 14.

12. Pike, *Op. cit.*, p. 167.

13. *Ibid.*, p. 208.

14. *Ibid.*, pp. 206-207.

15. *Ibid.*, pp. 295-296.

16. Brunner, H. Emil, Quoted by Paul King Jewett, "Emil Brunner's Conception of Revelation," in John F. Walvoord, Ed., *Inspiration And Interpretation*. Grand Rapids, Michigan: William B. Eerdmans Publishing Company, 1954, p. 110.

17. *Ahimon Rezon*, p. 91.

18. Pike, *Op. cit.*, p. 226.

19. Purkiser, W.T., *Exploring Our Christian Faith*. Kansas City, Missouri: Beacon Hill Press, 1960, p. 122.

20. Pike., *Op. cit.*, p. 160.

21. *Ibid.*, p. 166.

22. *Ibid.*, p. 225.

23. *Ibid.*, p. 167.

24. Purkiser, *Op. cit.*, p. 123.

25. *Ibid.*, p. 105.

26. Pike., *Op. cit.*, p. 524.

27. *Ibid.*, p. 625.

28. Steed, Ernest H. J., *Two Be One*. Copyright 1978 by Logos International, Reprinted by permission of Logos International Fellowship Incorporated, Plainfield, New Jersey,

07060.

29. Mohammad Maz-Hari, Address to Temple of Understanding Conference, New York, October 1924, 1975 — Quoted in Steed, Ernest H.J., *Two Be One*. p. 124. Reprinted by permission of Logos International Fellowship Incorporated, Plainfield, New Jersey, 07060.

30. Ferguson, Charles W., *Fifty Million Brothers*. New York: Farrar and Rinehart, Incorporated, 1937, p. 26.

Chapter 2: Occult and Kabalistic Connections

1. Niles, Daniel T., *The Preacher's Task and The Stone of Stumbling*. New York: Harper and Brothers, 1958, p. 99.

2. Pike, *Op. cit.*, p. 11.

3. Lindsell, Harold, *God's Incomparable Word*. Minneapolis, Minnesota: World Wide Publications, 1977, p. 117.

4. Pike, *Op. cit.*, p. 266.

5. Mackey, *Op. cit.*, "Scriptures," Vol. II, p. 672.

6. Pike, *Op. cit.*, p. 17.

7. Wilson, Colin, *The Occult — A History*. New York: Random House, 1971, p. 203.

8. Pike. *Op. cit.*, p. 741.

9. *Ibid.*, p. 625.

10. *Ibid.*, p. 266.

11. *Ibid.*, p. 17.

12. *Ibid.*, p. 745.

13. Baskin, Wade, *The Sorcerer's Handbook*. New York: Philosophical Library, 1974, p. 113.

14. Brooks, Patricia O., *The Return of the Puritans*. Skyland, North Carolina: New Puritan Library, 1979, p. 60.

15. Pike, *Op. cit.*, p. 745.

16. Wilson, *Op. cit.*, p. 209.

17. Spence, Lewis, "Kabala," *An Encyclopedia of Occultism,* Secaucus, New Jersey: University Books, 1960. p. 241.

18. Hill, Douglas and Pat Williams, *The Supernatural.* New York, Hawthorne Books, 1965, p. 144.

19. Pike, *Op. cit.*, p. 818.

20. *Ibid.*, p. 321.

21. *Ibid.*, p. 625-626.

22. *Ibid.*, p. 839.

23. *Ibid.*, p. 267.

24. *Ibid.*, p. 744.

25. *Ibid.*, p. 105.

26. Epstein, Perle, *The Way of Witches.* Garden City, New York: Doubleday and Company, 1972, p. 98.

Chapter 3: Religious Teachings of Masonry

1. Heckethorn, Charles William, *The Secret Societies of All Ages and Countries.* Secaucus, New Jersey: University Books, 1965, Vol. II, p. 109.

2. Rongstad, L. James, *"How to Respond to the Lodge."* St. Louis, Missouri: Concordia Publishing House, 1977, p. 13.

3. Mackey, *Op. cit.*, p. 619.

4. Pike, *Op. cit.*, p. 161.

5. *Ibid.*, p. 213.

6. *Ibid.*, p. 219.

7. *Ibid.*, p. 718.

8. *Ibid.*, p. 219.

9. *Ibid.*, p. 526.

10. *Ibid.*, p. 102.

11. *Ibid.*, p. 859.

12. Trueblood, D. Elton, *Philosophy of Religion*. New York: Harper and Brothers, 1957, p. 264.

13. Pike, *Op. cit.*, p. 321.

14. Hislop, *Op. cit.*, p. 277.

15. *Ibid.*, p. 278.

16. *Ibid.*, p. 279.

17. Letheridge, T.C., *Witches*. New York: Citidell Press, 1962, p. 46.

18. Hislop, *Op. cit.*, p. 280.

19. Pike, *Op. cit.*, p. 23.

20. *Ibid.*, p. 734.

21. Lyons, Arthur, *The Second Coming*, New York: Dodd, Mead, and Company, 1970, p. 32.

22. Bulfinch, Thomas, *Bulfinch's Mythology*. New York: Thomas Y. Crowell Company, 1947, p. 32.

23. Hislop, *Op. cit.*, p. 311.

24. DeGivry, Grillot, *Witchcraft, Magic and Alchemy*. New York: Dover Publications Incorporated, 1971, p. 75.

25. Spence, *Op. cit.*, p. 63.

26. Muller, W. Max, *The Mythology of All Races*. New York: Cooper Square Publishers Incorporated, 1964, Vol. XII, p. 164.

27. DeGivry, *Op. cit.*, p. 78.

28. Pike, *Op. cit.*, p. 308.

29. Rongstad, *Op. cit.*, p. 10.

30. Pike, *Op. cit.*, p. 137.

31. Rongstad, *Op. cit.*, p. 24.

32. Pike, *Op. cit.*, p. 540.

33. *Ibid.,* p. 719.

34. *Ibid.,* p. 310.

35. *Ibid.,* p. 525.

36. *Ibid.,* p. 308.

37. *Ibid.,* p. 525.

38. *Ibid.,* p. 62.

39. Steed, *Op. cit.,* p. 124. Reprinted by permission of Logos International Fellowship Inc., Plainfield, New Jersey, 07060.

Chapter 4: Deceptive Symbols

1. Achtemeier, Elizabeth, *The Feminine Crisis in Christian Faith.* New York: Abingdon Press, 1965, p. 99.

2. Pike, *Op. Cit.,* p. 819.

3. Hislop, *Op. cit.,* p. 5.

4. Bainton, *Op. cit.,* p. 76.

5. Pike, *Op. cit.,* p. 77.

6. *Ibid.,* p. 139.

7. *Ibid.,* p. 738.

8. *Ibid.,* p. 64.

9. *Ibid.,* p. 209.

10. *Ibid.,* p. 139.

11. *Ibid.,* p. 401.

12. Mackey, *Op cit.,* p. 560.

13. *Ibid.,* p. 573.

14. Mackey, Albert, *The Manual of the Lodge,* Quoted in McQuaig, Rev. Cecil F., ''The Masonic Report.'' Answer Books and Tapes, 5166 Old Norcross Road, Norcross, Georgia, 30071, p. 22-23.

15. Mackey, Albert, *Symbolism in Freemasonry,* Quoted in McQuaig, Rev. Cecil, F., "The Masonic Report." Answer Books and Tapes, 5166 Old Norcross Road, Norcross, Georgia, 30071, p. 22.

16. *Ibid.,* p. 22.

17. *Ibid.,* p. 22.

18. Albert Pike, quoted by Blavatsky, "Isis Unveiled," in Rev. Cecil McQuaig, ed., "The Masonic Report," p. 21.

19. Pike, *Op. cit.,* p. 402.

20. *Ibid.,* p. 15.

21. *Ibid.,* p. 771.

22. *Ibid.,* p. 393.

23. *Ibid.,* pp. 14-15.

24. Baskin, *Op. cit.,* p. 453.

25. *Ibid.,* p. 455.

26. *Ibid.,* p. 457.

27. Spence, *Op. cit.,* p. 262.

28. Stillson, Henry Leonard and William James Jughan, *History of the Ancient and Honorable Fraternity of Free and Accepted Masons.* Boston and New York: The Fraternity Publishing Company, 1902, p. 49.

29. Hill, *Op. cit.,* p. 144.

30. Pike, *Op. cit.,* p. 407.

31. Churchwood, James, *The Sacred Symbols of Mu.* New York: Paperback Library Incorporated, 1933, p. 99.

32. *Ibid.,* p. 101.

33. Stillson, *Op. cit.,* p. 45.

34. Pike, *Op. cit.,* p. 506.

35. *Ibid.,* p. 105.

36. *Ibid.,* p. 730.

37. *Ibid.*, p. 732.

38. *Ibid.*, p. 787.

Chapter 5: Self-Destructive Oaths

1. Nagel, Rev. Herman Kyle, *Finding Meaning in the Lord's Supper.* San Antonio, Texas: The Naylor Company, 1958, pp. 40-41.

2. Boude, William, *The Pilgrimage of Perfection,* quoted in the Masonic Bible, Philadelphia, Pennsylvania: A.J. Holman Company, 1957, p. 34.

3. Stevens, *Op. cit.,* pp. 19-20.

4. Whalen, William J., *Handbook of Secret Organizations.* Milwaukee, Wisconsin: The Bruce Publishing Company, 1966, p. 46.

5. Hislop, *Op. cit.,* p. 43.

6. *The Masonic Bible,* "A Masonic Creed." Philadelphia, Pennsylvania: A.J. Holman Company, 1957, p. 3.

7. Epstein, Perle, *The Way of Witches.* Garden City, New York: Doubleday and Company Incorporated, 1972, p. 42.

8. Whalen, *Op. cit.,* p. 57.

9. Epstein, *Op. cit.,* p. 99.

10. *King Solomon and His Followers.* 32 West 33rd Street, New York: Allen Publishing Company, 1943.

11. *Ibid.,* p. 25.

12. *Ibid.,* p. 114.

13. Whalen, *Op. cit.,* p. 61.

14. "Masonry in the Light of the Bible." Saint Louis, Missouri: Concordia Publishing House, 1954, p. 22.

15. Whalen, *Op. cit.,* p. 152.

16. *Ibid.,* pp. 155-156.

17. Rice, John R., *Lodges Examined by the Bible*. Murfreesboro, Tennessee: Sword of the Lord Publishers, 1943, pp. 24-25.

18. Pike, *Op. cit.*, p. 539.

19. *Ibid.*, p. 539.

20. Nagel, *Op. cit.*, p. ix.

21. Rice, *Op. cit.*, p. 78.

22. *Ibid.*, p. 78.

23. "Masonry in the Light of the Bible," p. 25.

Chapter 6: Come Out and Be Separate

1. Stevens, *Op. cit.*, p. 12.

2. Rice, *Op. cit.*, p. 79-80.

3. *Ibid.*, p. 55.

4. *Ibid.*, p. 75-76.

5. Pruess, Arthur, *Dictionary of Secret and Other Societies*. Saint Louis, Missouri: B. Herder Book Company, 1924, p. 143.

6. Stevens, *Op. cit.*, p. 12.

7. Encyclical Letter, "Praeclara Gratulationis Publicae," of June 20, 1894.

8. Rice, *Op. cit.*, p. 78.

Editor's Postlude

As this eleventh printing of *Should a Christian Be a Mason?* goes to press, God's judgments on the visible church have surely begun. Tinsel-and-glitter ministries, riddled with immorality and misuse of funds, are being exposed for the charlatans that they are. Also, the AIDS plague will surely strike down many millions before long. Will professing believers with loose morals be exempt or immune?

Revelation 17 and 18 describe the destruction of "Babylon the Harlot." Theories as to Babylon's identity abound, but the word means "confusion." What greater confusion can there be than for someone to worship the wrong god? When initiates of freemasonry declare themselves to be "seeking light," and turning from West to East, are they turning from Western Christianity to Eastern occultism? Will Almighty God, who punished ancient Israel for combining idolatry with His worship, wink at that same sin today?

Ancient Babylon was a headquarters of witchcraft and occultism, as well as for banking and economic totalitarianism. Can God's people today embrace Babylon's thinking without sharing her judgments?

Let us ponder carefully the verses in Revelation 17 and 18 which refer directly to believers:

"And I saw the woman drunken with the blood

of the saints, and with the blood of the martyrs of Jesus: and when I saw her, I wondered with great admiration" (Revelation 17:6).

"And I heard another voice from heaven, saying, Come out of her, my people, that ye be not partakers of her sins, and that ye receive not of her plagues" (Revelation 18:4).

" . . . for in one hour is she made desolate. Rejoice over her, thou heaven, and ye holy apostles and prophets; for God hath avenged you on her" (Revelation 18:19b and 20).

"And in her was found the blood of prophets, and of saints, and of all that were slain upon the earth" (Revelation 18:24).

Clear, isn't it? Either we get out of every abomination (i.e "partakers of her sins"), or we can expect to receive of her plagues. True, we may be martyred by the wicked while they still hold the reins of power before the King of kings comes. But which wrath would you rather face? The wrath of the wicked, which cannot outlast our earthly lives, or the wrath of a Holy God, who will banish the unrepentant to the lake of fire, for all eternity? (Revelation 2:11-15).

Time is surely running out for lining up all of life's decisions on this basis. Perhaps some of the other books mentioned in the next few pages will help some to decide God's way. But at least read the tract at the end of those pages, which summarizes the message of the Storms book so well. Feel free to photocopy those three pages, or have your own tract printed from them. Let us reach many with the truth while we still can.

Maranatha!

(Mrs.) Pat Brooks, NPL Editor

A BLOOD COVENANT IS THE MOST SOLEMN, BINDING AGREEMENT POSSIBLE BETWEEN TWO PARTIES.

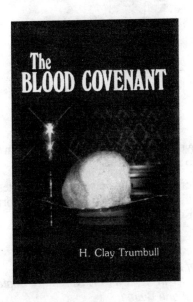

Perhaps one of the least understood, and yet most important and relevant factors necessary for an appreciation of the series of covenants and covenant relationships that our God has chosen to employ in His dealings with man, is the concept of the BLOOD COVENANT!

In this volume which has been "sold out," and "unavailable" for generations, lies truth which has blessed and will continue to bless every pastor, teacher, every serious Christian desiring to "go on with God."

Andrew Murray stated it beautifully years ago, when he said that if we were to but grasp the full knowledge of what God desires to do for us and understood the nature of His promises, it would "make the Covenant the very gate of heaven! May the Holy Spirit give us some vision of its glory."

$10.95 + 2.00 postage and handling

The
Acts
of
Pilate

ANCIENT RECORDS RECORDED BY
CONTEMPORARIES OF JESUS CHRIST
REGARDING THE FACTS CONCERNING
HIS BIRTH, DEATH, RESURRECTION

♦

TRANSLATED FROM THE ORIGINAL LANGUAGES
BY DRS. MCINTOSH and TWYMAN

♦

EDITED BY REV. W.D. MAHAN

This book was a favorite of the late Kathryn Kuhlman who often read from it on her radio show.

Early Church Writers such as Justin refer to the existence of these records, and Tertullian specifically mentions the report made by Pilate to the Emperor of Rome, Tiberius Caesar.

Chapters Include:
- *How These Records Were Discovered,*
- *A Short Sketch of the Talmuds,*
- *Constantine's Letter in Regard to Having Fifty Copies of the Scriptures Written and Bound,*
- *Jonathan's Interview with the Bethlehem Shepherds   Letter of Melker, Priest of the Synagogue at Bethlehem,*
- *Gamaliel's Interview with Joseph and Mary and Others Concerning Jesus,*
- *Report of Caiaphas to the Sanhedrim Concerning the Resurrection of Jesus,*
- *Valleus's Notes — "Acta Pilati," or Pilate's Report to Caesar of the Arrest, Trial, and Crucifixion of Jesus,*
- *Herod Antipater's Defense Before the Roman Senate in Regard to His Conduct At Bethlehem,*
- *Herod Antipas's Defense Before the Roman Senate in Regard to the Execution of John the Baptist,*
- *The Hillel Letters Regarding God's Providence to the Jews, by Hillel the Third*

THE ACTS OF PILATE $9.95, plus $2.00 Shipping

IMPACT CHRISTIAN BOOKS, INC.
332 Leffingwell Ave., Suite 101, Kirkwood, MO 63122

EXCITING NEW BOOK
ANSWERS AGE-OLD QUESTION

The author draws upon the Scriptural patterns and keys established by the Prophet Daniel to present readily understandable methods any believer can employ to *Tap into the Wisdom of God*. He shows from Scripture that it is both God's intention and will for man to turn to Him as the Source of knowledge.

You will learn seven major keys to receiving knowledge and find at least twenty-one practical encouragements to build your faith to seek God for answers.

Plus a Revelation

Discover for yourself the fascinating and prophetic secrets contained in Daniel Chapter Six, presented in the ninth chapter of this book. Chapter nine, which is actually a bonus book, presents an apparently undiscovered revelation showing more than one hundred parallels between Daniel and Jesus Christ.

"The most exciting thing I discovered was that what God did for Daniel, He can do for any believer!"

P.M., Bible Teacher, Kansas.

$10.95 + $1.50 Shipping

Impact Christian Books, Inc.
332 Leffingwell Ave., Suite 101,
Kirkwood, MO 63122

Christianity vs. Freemasonry

by James D. Shaw

In the U.S. 150 years ago, Freemasons were not permitted to belong to churches. If it were discovered that a church member was a Mason who refused to leave the lodge, he must leave the church. Freemasons found it difficult to survive in a country where they were limited to unchurched members for their lodges. Soon they tried to give Masonry a Christian mask. Freemasonry could not deny its deistic faith, but it could place a Bible on its altar and require a belief in God for all members. (It was not necessary for the candidate to specify which god!)

Few Christians realize that Freemasonry is a phallic cult. Webster's *New World Dictionary* makes it clear that the phallus is the image of the male reproductive organ, "worshiped as a symbol of generative power."

The *Encyclopedia of the Occult Sciences* states that Masonry teaches basic religion through symbols, belief in the Great Architect of the Universe, esoteric lore of alchemy, and the Kabala (ancient Hebrew sorcery-Ed.). Adept Masons state that their symbols were "deduced" from the Essenes and Druids, having been passed down from pre-flood days to Noah; then to Egyptians, Chaldeans, and masters in Israel.

Freemasonry is a world-wide conspiracy to destroy the Church of Jesus Christ on earth, a means to bring about a one-world church and government. With the Unitarian and Theosophical system in Masonry it is nearing this goal. Unsuspecting Christians, who do not know that Masonry is controlled by Satan, are also aiding it instead of exposing it.

Although the Roman Catholic Church officially condemns Masonry, 17 Masons are on the Vatican High Council. (Write ORCM, Inc., P.O. Box 542, Stratford, CT 06497.)

Mormonism has its roots deep in Freemasonry. Joseph Smith died giving a Masonic sign, "the grand hailing sign of distress." No Mormon believes he can enter heaven without these signs and grips and passwords.

The Illuminati, founded by Adam Weishaupt in 1776, spread their poison of worldwide revolution through freemasonry lodges. Karl Marx was paid by Nathan Rothschild, a European international banker, to put Weishaupt's ideas on paper for the masses. This document was the *Communist Manifesto.*

A founder of Soviet Bolshevism, C.G. Rakovsky, was one of the victims of the show trials under Stalin before World War II. To save his own life he offered to tell Illuminati secrets involving freemasonry in the world conspiracy. He told his captors "this great secret" which every Mason on earth should surely want to know:

"Every Masonic organization tries to attain and to create all the required prerequisites for the triumph of the Communist revolution . . . But since the Communist revolution has in mind the liquidation, as a class, of the whole bourgeosie, the physical destruction of all bourgeois rulers, it follows that *the real secret of masonry — is the suicide of Freemasonry as an organization, and the physical suicide of every more important Mason."* (From *Fourth Reich of the Rich,* by·Des Griffin, p. 254)

There you have it. Not only is freemasonry evil, but it is conspiring in a movement which seeks its destruction!

Freemasonry is also the worship of Lucifer. It is anti-Christ. The name of our dear Savior is never permitted to be used in any rite in all of free-masonry. In John 10:30 the Lord Jesus said, "I and the Father are one." Yet *the lodge leaves Jesus out.* How can a lodge member who professes to be a Christian enter a lodge that leaves Jesus and the Holy Spirit *out*? If he is a believer who has the Holy Spirit indwelling, should he not be fearful of grieving the Holy Spirit?

As a former 33rd degree Mason, I beg those in Masonry, the Eastern Star, and other secret societies to "come out from among them, and be ye separate, saith the Lord, and touch not the unclean thing; and I will receive you." (2 Cor. 6:18)

Rev. Jim Shaw
Box 844
Silver Springs, FL 32688

Permission is hereby granted for anyone to reprint this tract without changes, provided this credit line is included beneath the author's name and address:

Reprinted by permission of:
New Puritan Library, Inc.,
Fletcher, North Carolina 28732.

Those wanting help in being set free from bondage may contact Jim Shaw or:

HRT Ministries, Box 12, Newtonville, NY 12128
Free the Masons Ministries, P.O. Box 1077, Issaquah, WA 98027; or
Christian Truth & Victory, Route 5, Box 252-A, Alexandria, MN 56308

THE HEAVENS DECLARE . . .

William D. Banks

More than 250 pages!
More than 50 illustrations!

- Who named the stars and why?
- What were the original names of the stars?
- What is the secret message hidden in the stars?

The surprising, **secret message** contained in the earliest, original names of the stars, is revealed in this new book.

The deciphering of the star names provides a fresh revelation from the heart of **the intelligence** behind creation. Ten years of research includes material from the British Museum dating prior to 2700 B.C.

A clear explanation is given showing that early man had a sophisticated knowledge of One, True God!

$6.95 + $1.50 Shipping/Handling

ALIVE AGAIN!

William D. Banks

The author, healed over twenty years ago, relates his own story. His own testimony presents a miracle or really a series of miracles — as seen through the eyes of a doubting skeptic, who himself becomes the object of the greatest miracle, because he is Alive Again!

The way this family pursues and finds divine healing as well as a great spiritual blessing provides a story that will at once bless you, refresh you, restore your faith or challenge it! You will not be the same after you have read this true account of the healing gospel of Jesus Christ, and how He is working in the world today.

The healing message contained in this book needs to be heard by every cancer patient, every seriously ill person, and by every Christian hungering for the reality of God.

More than a powerful testimony — here is teaching which can introduce you or those whom you love to healing and to a new life in the Spirit!

$4.95 + $1.50 Shipping/Handling

Impac **Chris** **ian** **Books**

332 Leffingwell Ave., Suite 101
Kirkwood, MO 63122

AVAILABLE AT YOUR LOCAL BOOKSTORE, OR YOU MAY
ORDER DIRECTLY. Toll-Free, order-line only M/C, DISC,
or VISA 1-800-451-2708.

Write for *FREE* Catalog.